'It is so important in life to have role models and to be inspired by individuals who are each following their paths while spreading positive vibes everywhere they go. Through *Unpopular Culture*, Guvna B is doing just this. He is a young, talented man who is leading by example.'

Oliver Proudlock, reality TV star and founder of Serge DeNimes

'I love this book. I love it because the writing carries weight from Isaac's real-life experiences. He could be performing to ten thousand in an arena or a hundred in a youth-club basement, yet he will still plaster it all over social media and give everything he has got because he cares about the next generation. He does what he does for the broken teenager rather than the fame, popularity or credit. You will enjoy this book; it's raw, real and relevant to today's culture.'

Dan Blythe, Youth and Young Adults Pastor, Hillsong London

'Guvna B is a creative, credible and courageous voice to Millennials. I've seen him speak to huge crowds on stage through his music, and I've seen him speak off the stage, just as powerfully, into the lives of young people. Through the pages of this brilliant new book, he'll speak directly to you – telling you his story and encouraging you in yours. *Unpopular Culture* will help to refresh your world view, renew your mind – and cheer you on as you live with purpose and passion for Christ.'

Matt Redman, Grammy award-winning singer/songwriter

'I've known Guvna B for a while now and he is a very positive person. I'm confident that if you read his book, it will inspire you – and many other people too.'

Dion Dublin, former England footballer

D1080920

'Guvna B is a great example for the youth and a very knowledgeable guy. You'll love *Unpopular Culture*.'

Posty, GRM Daily

'Guvna B genuinely cares about making an impact on young people. His passion, drive and dedication are an inspiration. With *Unpopular Culture*, he has some good stuff to say, trust me.'

Naomi Scott, actress and singer

'This book will totally take you into the depths of who Guvna B is. He is so honest on his journey. While reading this book, I found so many similarities. This book will inspire you and bring clarity about what your purpose is. No matter which path you choose, Guvna B encourages you to be a light and shine wherever you go.'

Michelle Williams, Destiny's Child

'Guvna B has always stood out for me as being not only the kind of artist your parents would want you to listen to but also an artist most MCs would be scared to go toe to toe with. His music is a perfect balance of vibe, skill and deep messages, and a reflection of this book, so you'll definitely enjoy it.'

DJ Ace, BBC Radio 1Xtra

'Guvna B has an amazing way with words and always has done as an artist, so to have his brilliant, wise words in print is a must-have for anyone who needs positivity in their life.'

Alec Boateng, Head of A&R (Artists and Repertoire), Atlantic Records

'I've known Guvna B for a few years now but knew of his work before that. He is a man of the Church, yet reaches non-churchgoers because of his honest lyrics. That's not an easy challenge but Guvna does it effortlessly. *Unpopular Culture* showcases moral character, decency and humility. You'll love it!'

Richard Blackwood, actor and comedian

UNPOPULAR CULTURE

GUVNA B

First published in Great Britain in 2017

Society for Promoting Christian Knowledge
36 Causton Street
London SW1P 4ST
www.spck.org.uk

British Library Cataloguing-in-Publication Data
A catalogue record for this book is available from the British Library

ISBN 978-0-281-07631-4
eBook ISBN 978-0-281-07632-1

Typeset by Manila Typesetting Company
First printed in Great Britain by Jellyfish Solutions
Subsequently digitally printed in Great Britain

eBook by Manila Typesetting Company

Produced on paper from sustainable forests

Mum and Dad.

Thanks for the love and the sacrifices.
I am who I am because of how you raised me.

Thank you.

CONTENTS

INTRODUCTION

Every single person on this planet is completely unique. From our hair colour to our different interests, the way we move our feet to the way we structure our sentences, we're all entirely different. I'm reminded of this daily from my upbringing in London, one of the most diverse places in the world, bringing together a multitude of different cultures, races and ethnicities in one city. However, despite being fully aware of my individuality, I still struggle with the desire to fit in. This shaped me when I was growing up, and even now I find myself trying to conform, and I know I'm not alone.

We live in a culture where it's becoming more and more common – and even encouraged – to put pressure on our friends, make people feel insecure, gossip, bully, and abuse drugs, alcohol and sex. If you're not buying into this way of life, you can become unpopular, and being unpopular often leaves us feeling cut off from society.

When I look at the city in which I live, its culture and way of life don't fill me with much confidence either. I continually hear of stabbings and shootings, and suicide and self-harm are increasingly prevalent. I see girls being disrespected by guys, and the majority of people appear to be focused on money and material possessions. Countless TV channels are filled with reality shows that encourage self-loathing: we watch others alter their physical appearance in search of the perfect body, as we question our own.

Why is it popular to do these things, behave in these ways or hold these views? Could it be that we're all buying into the same story and the same way of doing things, just because we don't know any different? Have we just followed what we've picked up from life experiences and the examples of people around us?

I think we can do so much better than the standard of society we've allowed to become the norm. Let's not settle with being products of our culture, reflecting the same values and desires as the masses around us. Let's not succumb to the status quo, fitting into the stereotypes others assign to us. We're game-changers, revolution-makers, instigators. Popular culture has had the limelight for too long. It's time for unpopular culture to take the stage.

CHAPTER 1

COUNCIL ESTATE OF MIND

I'm east London born and bred. My parents grew up in Ghana and then came over to England in their mid-twenties in search of a better life. Little Guvna came along shortly afterwards, and they did their best to provide me with everything I needed to reach my full potential. As a rap artist, I've often thought that my love for words was established in me by my parents. They used encouraging words to communicate to me the endless possibilities life could bring. My dad would often pray for me, and my mum would pray with me. I remember vividly how their words of faith and hope would make me feel moved and uplifted. Though we didn't have much, I was an ambitious little boy who wasn't fazed by my reality.

I grew up on a council estate in Custom House, east London. It's pretty close to where they held the Olympics in 2012, so nowadays it's considered quite a sought-after location. Now that the golden feet of athletes like Usain Bolt have walked its streets, they've knocked down a lot of the old Custom House council blocks and built fancy apartments. It used to be very different when I was a youngster. The majority of people who grew up around me on the estate lacked real ambition. I say *real* ambition, because we always had *some* kind of desire to do well in life, but our motivation to aspire was fuelled by the wrong things. We had what I would call a 'council estate of mind'. Our benchmark for success was how impressive the local drug dealer's car was, or which of the native gang members had the most respect.

I remember when I was about eight and I was doing some kick-ups on a plot of grass outside my council block. This was back when jumpers were goalposts and vending-machine Freddos were 10p. The internet was a dial-up connection, which meant that you could be waiting for anything up to five minutes for a Google search to load. None of us could afford phone credit so we had to go to our friends' houses and actually knock for them. Forty pence could get you on a bus and Super Mario and Crash Bandicoot were the most popular names on the block. Ah . . . the good old days. Anyway, back to my story.

The most popular crew on our patch were playing a football match at the other end of the green. This was one of the most feared gangs on the estate. The rumours that flew around about them were enough to give most people nightmares. I was doing my kick-ups far enough away from them to stay out of trouble, but close enough for them to acknowledge my existence. I was minding my own business when one of the boys kicked their football over in my direction by accident. I looked at them, then looked at the ball, then looked back at them. My poor little insecure, fearful, eight-year-old brain couldn't figure out whether to pretend that I hadn't seen the ball, pick it up and kick it back over to them, or just run home as fast as my young legs could carry me. This predicament lasted at most about 20 seconds, but in that time I had managed to conjure up various scenarios in my mind.

If I pick it up and chuck it back over there will they be furious that I touched their property? If I pretend I didn't see the ball will they know that I'm lying? In returning the ball, what if I miskick it in a completely unintended direction? Manchester United players do that *all* the time.

I was petrified. However, just before I had to come to a decision, one of the lads shouted, 'Yo, Isaac. Pass the ball, bruv. Nice one.'

My jaw dropped. 'Wow. They know my name,' I said to myself. Absolutely delighted, I passed the ball back and walked home with the biggest smile on my face.

Whenever I think back to that story, I'm embarrassed at how I behaved. I had found fulfilment in being accepted by a group of individuals who didn't care about me. I felt successful because teenagers who stood for everything I thought I stood against acknowledged me. Though I was only eight years old, early life experiences like this eventually sent me down a very unsatisfying path of worthless endeavours. I turned to money, girls, cars and clothes to try and find fulfilment. Those things satisfied for a moment but couldn't satisfy me for ever. I'd always find myself searching for the next thrill or the next buzz. I had unknowingly become a product of my environment.

I was fortunate enough to have Christian parents who encouraged me to draw near to God. It was touch and go for most of my teenage years but I came to realise that I had free access to something a great deal more valuable than the things I was chasing in my clouded council estate of mind. A caring Saviour wears the scars of my freedom. He loves and accepts me unconditionally, and in the years that I've known that to be true I've struggled to find anything that satisfies me more. Although Hebrews 11.1 might assure me now that 'faith is the substance of things hoped for, the evidence of things not seen' (AV), when I was growing up I struggled to see beyond my circumstances because I had no hope and no assurance. I aspired to acquire the things that I saw with my natural eyes. Now knowing God has inspired me to hope for more than the material, more than the immediate, and to be assured that God has greater things planned for me than I could ever imagine.

CHAPTER 2

WHO AM I?

My mother always told me that if I knew who I was, I'd be just fine. A pithy soundbite like that may sound amazing, but I didn't understand what 'knowing myself' actually meant. Or, for that matter, how I could achieve it.

Finding out who we truly are is a quest many of us embark on; some struggle, some don't. For me, it's always been a concept I've found hard to get to grips with. Many of my friends have gone travelling around the world to 'find themselves'. Perhaps there is a secret undercover location in remote Thailand that stores the real versions of ourselves, just waiting to be discovered by Western gap-year travellers.

I didn't go down that route. Instead, unintentionally, I chose trial and error. And much closer to home.

Black Del Boy

In my first attempt to find out who I truly was, I pursued cold, hard cash. From the tender age of 12, I learned the art of profiteering. I'd buy a multipack of sweets for £1 and then sell each individual packet in school at a marked-up price. For every £1 invested in sugar I'd make £2 profit in coins. I took home around £10 a week, which wasn't too bad for someone not yet in their teens. However, fast-forward a couple of years and that weekly tenner just wasn't cutting it for me any more. I wanted more; I needed a more profitable hustle.

Out of all my friends I was probably the most obsessed with music, always the first to listen to newly released albums and singles. I had a portable CD player that fit just perfectly inside the side pocket of my blazer. It wasn't the best design – it used to skip songs every time I ran or made a sudden movement – but it meant that I always had the latest music playing on my way to and from class. I soon realised that there was a demand for new music in school, and hit upon a fresh financial scheme.

At home I would curate a mix of all the latest songs, burning them on to cheap blank CDs. I'd choose the best R&B, hip-hop and UK garage tracks, and fit as many on to a disc as possible. I'd then sell the CDs at break-time for £5. On a good day I'd make upwards of £40 *and* boost my reputation as the finest music connoisseur in year nine. The whole operation was obviously illegal, as I didn't have permission from any of the music artists to use their songs, but hopefully I'll never get in trouble for it as I didn't know any better at the time. Anyway, the money went towards feeding my desires for the latest trainers or name brand clothes.

Whatever weird and wonderful ways there were to make money, I was all in. I called it business acumen, but most called me the 'black Del Boy'. Although I'd found some skill in being a young trader, I soon realised that it didn't really solve any of my deep-rooted problems or give me the satisfaction I had so greatly anticipated. I turned my attention to other interests, such as girls, clothes and cars, but I found similar feelings of dissatisfaction. My teenage romances would break down as we discovered we were imperfect people looking for perfection. My love for cars and clothes left me feeling frantic, struggling to keep up with ever-changing trends. I was discovering that placing my identity in imperfect people or impermanent things meant that in losing those, I'd lose myself.

Eagle in a Pigeonhole

In a culture that is so quick to define people by labels and place people in boxes, how do we know what our true identity is? Often we're defined by the relationships we have with others, our skin colour, where we're from, educational achievements, or our occupation. I've been a professional rap artist for nearly ten years, but when I started out I never made a concrete decision about what genre of music I was creating. I just picked up a pen and, as ink met paper, out flowed honest lyrics about my life.

When I became a Christian, it completely changed my world view. I would rap about my faith in Jesus as well as addressing everyday issues from a Christian viewpoint. Before I knew it, people labelled me as a 'Gospel artist'. I didn't have an issue with that; in fact I started to embrace the label.

However, I soon realised that this label often resulted in me being put in a very tight, inflexible pigeonhole. I remember being offered an incredible opportunity with one of the UK's top mainstream radio stations. They had come across one of my songs and loved how positive and uplifting it was, and invited me to perform at an event in Cardiff. I was really looking forward to it, but a few days before the event they emailed saying that the event management had just found out that I was a Gospel artist and they feared that this could put people off attending the gig. They cancelled my appearance.

I was understandably disappointed, but as well as disappointment I felt real frustration. I was aware of this gift God had blessed me with and I was ready to spread my wings and fly with it, but I was unable to. The radio station had loved my song and wanted me to perform, but when they heard about the label I'd been pasted with, they no longer desired to move forward. They placed me in a 'Gospel artist' box and this box limited what I was able to do, where I was allowed to perform and who I could impact with my music.

The Bible says in John 8.36 that 'if the Son sets you free, you will be free indeed' (NIV). This means that the labels others place on us don't have to hold us captive. Though others may have a perception of our limitations, the Bible shows us that we can take on an attitude of freedom. I believe that labels are for items and boxes are for products and we are so much more than that. God didn't create us to be limited by the expectations of others. He created us out of his great love, to enjoy all that he is and all he has done, and so that we can be part of his eternal plan.

We are God's workmanship, created in Christ Jesus to do good works, which God prepared in advance for us to do. (Ephesians 2.10, NIV)

This verse says that God has prepared great things for us to do. I don't know any human who knows the complete mind of God, which must mean that there are some things that God has planned for us that people who put us in boxes may not know about. It's not that we are not *able* to do all those things within these boxes, but it is much more impactful if we act with the freedom that has been made available to us through Jesus. Don't let others dictate your limitations; live outside the box.

Pick Up the Manual

In 1 Samuel 16.7 it reads: 'man looks on the outward appearance, but the LORD looks on the heart' (ESV). God's view of success is very different from how the world views success. We may look at a person's job, exam results, or attractiveness to deem how successful they are, but the Bible says that God looks at the heart. He doesn't define us by how we look or what we do. Your 'do' is not your 'who'.

Deep down in my heart, I've genuinely found that the only thing worth placing my identity in is something perfect, unchanging and unconditional. Jesus is all of these things and more. Colossians 2.10 says, 'in Christ you have been brought to fullness'. Fullness can be described as 'being filled to capacity' or 'lacking nothing'. That sounds like something solid in which I can place my identity.

I've found the search for my true identity is kind of like how I am with a new electronic appliance. As soon as I get the new gadget home, I get it out of the packaging and throw the box over to the other side of the room. I think to myself, 'This can't be *that* hard to use,' and I proceed to try and figure it out with manly determination. After wasting hours attempting to get it working properly I eventually admit defeat and turn to YouTube, watching endless – and differing – tutorials on how to assemble the said appliance correctly. Some of the videos

are incredibly long and then don't even have the answers
I'm looking for. Finally, I take the short walk of shame over to
the other side of the room, pick up the box and take out the
manual. After all, I admit weakly in defeat, the best advice I
am going to find is from the original creator.

We are the creation and God is the creator. He knows how we
work best and so we can have full faith putting our identity in
him. He will never, ever let us down. This doesn't mean that
we can't enjoy other things, it just means that we shouldn't
allow other things to define us. I don't think there's a problem
with us having things; I think there's a problem with things
having us.

How do we know where our identity lies? Well, that's a tough
question but here's a start. Think about all the possessions
you own or the hobbies you currently do. If you were to wake
up tomorrow and they had all been taken away from you,
you would understandably be upset, but would it change
who you are as a person? If your identity is in the right place,
you'll know that even if you lose it all, there is still hope. You
also know that even if you never get it back, you still have a
purpose and you're still loved. This is what I have learnt from
reading God's manual, the Bible.

But putting full faith in God is totally counter-cultural and
often easier said than done.

CHAPTER 3

POPULAR CULTURE BEHIND THE SCENES

I'll be the first to admit that in school, college and university, I didn't pay as much attention as I should have. I was more interested in getting people to like me, or daydreaming about all the things I could do outside of the classroom to be more successful. I was more focused on profit than protractors and cash rather than compasses. I often found teachers boring and couldn't see how the information we were being taught would be relevant to my future. Looking back, there is definitely some truth in those thoughts, but in actual fact a lot of what I learned in school was really valuable. One thing that kept me engaged was learning about 'the seven dimensions of wellness'. In simplified terms, wellness is all about the different aspects of life that make life what it is. It's about becoming aware and making choices towards a healthier and more fulfilling life.

The theory behind it places us in the middle, with areas of 'wellness' surrounding us: social, emotional, spiritual, environmental, occupational, intellectual and physical. In easier terms, these relate to our interactions with people. Social wellness is how we positively connect with others. Emotional wellness is how we cope with the challenges life can bring. Spiritual wellness is where we find our peace. Environmental wellness is the part we play in our communities and our world. Occupational wellness can be described as the fulfilment we get from our jobs. Intellectual wellness is the ability to open our minds to new ideas, and physical wellness is based on maintaining a healthy quality of life.

Whether we're intentional about it or not, these various aspects of wellness are very much apparent in all of our lives. For me, while studying the topic, it became clear that God viewed each dimension completely differently from how they were seen by the culture I was a part of. The things that popular culture promoted had nothing in common with what God championed. What popular culture showed me seemed appetising and fulfilling, while what I saw of God seemed mundane and empty. However, as I began to follow the path the world had laid out, I found – to my disappointment – that not all that glittered was gold. In the next few chapters, I'm going to take you through just a few of the dimensions that really helped me look at my life differently.

A Stranger to Myself

I was a relatively new Christian when I left home and went to study for my Business and Journalism degree at the University of Hertfordshire. At that point in my life, God had my heart and I felt relatively satisfied and fulfilled with the new life that I had chosen to live. At home in London I had like-minded people around me who shared similar views on faith, and I had become friends with a few down-to-earth Christians I could actually relate to. Before that, I'd thought Christians were generally weird and socially awkward. I remember going up to one of my youth leaders when I was 13 years old and saying, 'Hi, how you doing?' and getting a reply something along the lines of, 'By the grace of the Lord, I'm blessed and highly favoured.' I remember thinking to myself, 'Who says stuff like that in normal conversation?!'

You can imagine my delight when I met Christians who dressed like me, spoke like me, and listened to UK garage just like me! I was ecstatic and life was good. And then I got to university.

Chauffeured by my emotional parents, I recall arriving on campus nervously excited about the prospect of meeting new people and being away from home. As I approached my halls of residence, I met one of my new flatmates who let me know that all the new arrivals were going to congregate in the kitchen at 8 p.m. to get to know each other. It seemed like a good idea, so I confirmed my attendance and headed to my room with my parents to start unpacking my suitcases. Before we knew it, it was approaching 8 p.m., and I waved my parents away and headed towards the kitchen to meet the other students in my block. With every step the sound of music and laughter got louder and louder. I strolled in and there they were: my seven flatmates having the time of their lives. What I presumed usually resembled a normal kitchen had been turned into a mix between an off-licence and a nightclub. I loved my flatmates. They were really cool people and we got on really well, but it was certainly a different environment compared with what I was used to.

As a Christian who had spent the last few months building a relationship with God and refocusing on what was really important for my life, I found being the odd one out – in a situation like my first day at university – a real culture shock. It was an unfamiliar way of life with a set of attitudes I hadn't really been exposed to in great detail before. Growing up on a council estate and going to school in London meant that I wasn't completely oblivious to the things I witnessed, but being at university definitely exposed that lifestyle in a much more explicit way.

And so I struggled. I struggled with being around people who weren't like me. I struggled with seeing people who had more money than me, even if they attained it in ways I didn't agree with. I struggled with seeing my peers having more thrills and excitement in their lives than I did. I struggled with being unpopular. Because of those struggles, I compromised who I was and started to adopt the way of life that the people around me so happily advertised. I didn't care what it cost me, I just wanted to be accepted. I aspired to fit in, but often fitting in means getting lost in the crowd. I was a stranger to myself.

I once watched a Will Smith interview where he said, 'Too many people are buying things they can't afford, with money that they don't have, to impress people that they don't like.' That quote sums up what uni culture sold to me, and I bought it with my last pound.

Mind Control

God's view on our social lives couldn't be more different from what I picked up at university. Romans 12.2 (ESV) says this: 'Do not be conformed to this world, but be transformed by the renewal of your mind, that by testing you may discern what is the will of God, what is good and acceptable and perfect.'

The mind is an interesting thing because, in and of itself, it's neutral. But once it's influenced and informed by an evil principle, it becomes an instrument of evil. In the same way, if it's influenced and informed by a good principle, it becomes an instrument of good. For the most part, from as early as I can remember the world I grew up in influenced me to make as much money as possible, get as many girls as possible, and to put myself first. This is what my mind was conditioned to go after. Not many people realise that we can actually choose our thoughts and take control of the things that pass through our mind. For me, 'renewing my mind' meant being intentional about the things that I thought about. If we're *not* intentional, our minds will subconsciously fill with everything the world feeds us.

Date Night

At the time Emma and I met, I wasn't looking for a girlfriend. I had had a few relationships that didn't work out and at that point I was more focused on developing my character and being a better person. One day I decided to catch up with my friend Ben, who I hadn't seen for a few months. He asked how things were going on the girls front and I said, 'Nothing much, I haven't come across anyone I really like in a while. If you find anyone let me know.' He said he'd have a think. I was half joking, so I wasn't expecting to hear anything from him on the subject. But a few days later he texted me saying he might have found me the perfect match. He sent me a picture of Emma Francis. I replied with something like 'Phwwwooaaaar, she's kinda nice innit?' He replied, 'I heard she likes hip-hop and grime music too.' I liked the sound of that so I asked him to get me her number. A few minutes later, he sent it through and I saved it in my phone.

A few days later I was at a music festival called Hackney Weekend. My phone vibrated and when I looked at it I saw there was a text from Emma. 'Hi, I just got a call from this number. Who's this?' Like a complete doughnut, I had put my phone in my pocket without locking it and it had somehow managed to call her. The main reason I was so disappointed in myself was because I always thought I was the coolest of smooth operators. She probably thought differently! Anyway, I somehow managed to salvage the situation, and after exchanging texts for a few weeks, I asked her out on a date.

We went to an Italian restaurant and the conversation flowed well because we had a lot in common. We were both Christians and we both loved food, music, and helping young people reach their full potential. After a great meal, I offered to drive her home and she accepted. It happened to be the same night they were opening The Shard, Europe's tallest building. As we were walking to my car we came across a grand celebration of the event with a large crowd and incredible fireworks and she loved it. Obviously I told her I had planned for us to walk that route so she could see it all, but in reality I had no idea it was happening! We spoke more in the car and the good vibes continued. As we turned into her road, I started thinking about how to make the 'goodnight' as smooth as possible. The conversation in my head went a little something like this.

ME: She must have had a good time?

INNER ME: Of course she has, she's with you.

ME: Yeah, true.

INNER ME: She might actually like you. Don't do anything stupid.

ME: OK. We're pulling up to her house. Shall I walk her to the door?

INNER ME: This isn't a film, mate. Chill out. Just tell her you've had a good night.

ME: OK, cool, shall I go in for a hug?

INNER ME: Yeah, why not? Give her the Christian one, though. You know, the one where you tap them on the back twice to show you're just friends?

ME: How about a kiss?

INNER ME: Nope, you've just had Italian food. Garlic alert.

ME: OK, cool, a hug it is.

As we stopped outside her house, Emma said how much of a good night she'd had and how she'd like to do it again some time. Pleased with her feedback, I reached over to give her a hug but by the time I had moved towards her, the passenger door was open and she was out of there. In one of the most embarrassing moments of my life, there I was, reached over with an arm half extended feeling like a complete idiot. I could hear 'inner me' laughing his head off. I looked left and right to make sure nobody saw the rejection, and then put the pedal to the floor.

When I got home that night, and the embarrassment had faded away, I was strangely content. I may have missed out on a hug, but that night was the beginning of a friendship that resulted in me marrying someone I've promised to spend the rest of my life with.

True Love Finds a Way

I asked Emma to officially be my girl a few months after and our families were really happy for us both. Emma's granddad, George, even wrote me a letter giving me his blessing. The reason I'm telling you this is because in this letter he gave me various bits of advice, and he finished it off with 'and remember . . . true love finds a way.' Those last five words have stayed with me ever since and have become the motto for our marriage. It's even engraved on the inside of my wedding ring.

The need for instant satisfaction means that it's not uncommon for people to move on when someone or something better comes along. Social media can be a highlights reel. We mostly see only the exciting parts of people's lives online, and that means that the grass can always look greener on the other side. The world is constantly feeding us messages and images of what life is meant to be about or what we need to make us happy. Money, a new car, plastic surgery, a big house, the list goes on. For that reason, we can take for granted what we already have, in the search for something more thrilling. To add to that, life isn't always plain sailing. Difficult times will come and they will test our resolve. Whether we're finding it hard to be understood, stressed with trying to get the grades we want, or struggling to pay our bills, in hard situations, giving up can sometimes seem like a great option.

I think what Granddad George was hinting at is that there are temptations in life and there are tough times. And although culture around us may subconsciously lead us to think and act in certain ways, we can choose whether or not to act on these thoughts. If you've truly committed to love someone, when those rough moments come or you're faced with the lure of something that looks more exciting, you can choose not to get distracted. Instead you hang in there and you choose to stick together as a team no matter what. True love is a choice, and if it is taken seriously there will always be a way to make it through.

The Gift of Giving

Another thing I chose to think about more was people in less fortunate situations than me. I remember the first time I really took the time to speak to a homeless person. I strolled past him outside Piccadilly tube station on a chilly winter's afternoon. He was wearing a dirty T-shirt with a pretty worn-out jacket over the top of it. His trousers were clearly too short for him, revealing that he had no socks on – just a pair of old trainers. As I walked past, I thought to myself, 'He must be freezing'. I carried on walking, but heard a clear voice in my head telling me to go back and speak to him. At first I ignored the voice, but I just couldn't shake it, so I turned around and went over to him. I asked his name, and how his day was going. I simply had a conversation with him, telling him a bit about myself, and finding out about his dreams and aspirations. After our chat, he didn't ask me for anything but I walked over to the local café anyway and bought him a sausage and bacon sandwich. When I handed it to him, he explained that while he appreciated the sandwich and it was a lovely gesture, most of all he was grateful that out of the thousands of people who had hurried by him that day, I was the only one to stop and treat him like a human being. To know that I had helped him feel that way made that day one of my most satisfying on earth.

In a world that had taught me that fulfilment comes from taking as much as I could and looking out for number one, it's crazy to think that this feeling of satisfaction came from a simple act of giving. The society I was a part of would describe a quality social life as having friends who are just as successful as you, sleeping around with various people as and when the feeling takes you, putting yourself first, and trusting no one. I've found it wise to have a range of friends: some who are further along than you so you can learn from them, and some who are behind you so you can teach them. I've also found it inspiring to be in a meaningful marriage, rather than investing time and effort into getting as many girls as possible. I've found it comforting to give rather than to take, and to trust people who care about me. Alone we may go faster, but together we will go further.

CHAPTER 4

REAL MEN DON'T CRY

On my childhood estate there always seemed to be an endless stream of bad news. Shootings, stabbings, armed robberies, death by drug or alcohol misuse, fatherlessness – and all this coupled with the bad news on the TV too. I still remember coming home after school on 11 September 2001 and seeing footage of the heartbreaking terror attacks in New York. All this negativity desensitised me so I became unable to express real emotion, and it played a damaging part in the relationships I had. My friends and family often described me as blasé, uninterested and having a heart of stone.

I don't know what comes to your mind when you hear the word 'emotion'. Maybe you think of someone crying or a need to care for someone in need. The truth is, I never really thought about my emotions and how I expressed them because I didn't really know I had to. The way I coped with painful situations in my life was to generally get over them. It was easier when I was growing up because painful times often centred on fairly minor issues such as not being picked for a football team, or being left out of a friendship group. It got much harder to deal with my emotions when I was a little older because difficult situations had a bigger impact on my life.

Lightning Strikes

My earliest memory of being noticeably emotionally affected was one rainy day in year eight. My friends and I looked forward to lunchtime at my secondary school because for a whole uninterrupted hour we were able to play football. We were kicking a ball about in the deserted playground. All the other students had run inside to find shelter, but for some reason the torrential rain didn't faze us. We carried on playing when, out of nowhere, a sudden lightning bolt struck the middle of the playground. We all fell to the floor, startled by the sheer power of it.

I was in a daze for about 20 seconds, then I staggered to my feet while trying to process the complete shock of what had just happened. I looked around and to one side of me I saw one of my friends, Joe, stumbling to his feet; over to the other side of me another boy also stood up. However, when I looked ahead to the middle of the playground, I saw one of my good mates, Issy, lying lifeless on the concrete. Before we had time to take in what had just happened, we sprinted over to check if he was OK. As we got closer, it soon became clear that he wasn't. There were burn marks and holes all over his school blazer, shirt and trousers. He was unconscious and unresponsive, and that's when we realised that the lightning had actually struck him, gone through his body and then hit the ground. A few kids ran inside to get a teacher and the rest of us stood there in complete and utter disbelief. Our head of year came rushing out and desperately tried to resuscitate him. Despite his attempts, there were no signs of life. Then the ambulance turned up and paramedics wasted no time in using a defibrillator to try and revive Issy. After what seemed like an age, they managed to get a pulse. They placed an oxygen mask over his face, and rushed him to hospital in a critical but stable condition.

By God's grace and after several months, Issy made a full recovery, but the repercussions of what happened were long-lasting for me. I was deeply concerned for my friend but I had no idea how to express my feelings. I was raised in a culture that taught me that 'real men don't cry' and so I did everything within my power not to, believing that a lack of tears proved my strength.

Breaking My Heart

I remember the first time I realised that my emotional well-being was an issue. A few years ago I made a worship music playlist that I could play in the mornings to keep me focused and in the right frame of mind for the day ahead. A song by Hillsong United called 'Hosanna' came on and the lyrics of the final verse struck a deep chord with me.

Heal my heart and make it clean
Open up my eyes to the things unseen
Show me how to love like You have loved me
Break my heart for what breaks Yours
Everything I am for Your Kingdom's cause
As I walk from earth into eternity.

I remember thinking, 'Wow, can God actually be broken-hearted?' I guess I subconsciously forgot that God was real and that he has feelings and emotions. I so often looked at him as a genie or as a distant father that I could occasionally talk to. I was moved to dig deep into the Bible, and came across a passage in Luke that really transformed the way I thought about God: 'Now as He drew near, He saw the city and wept over it, saying, "If you had known, even you, especially in this your day, the things that make for your peace! But now they are hidden from your eyes"' (Luke 19.41–42, NKJV).

So check this out. Jesus was walking into Jerusalem at this point and he was *the man*. A lot of people respected him and he was drawing a crowd everywhere he went. Imagine arriving at your local shopping centre having just scored the winning goal for your country in the World Cup – Jesus was receiving that sort of attention as he walked through Jerusalem. People were cheering for him, but Jesus was crying. The Saviour of the world was an emotional wreck! But why? Because he knew that the same people who were cheering him on at that precise moment would be campaigning to have him crucified very soon. He knew that Judas, someone he loved and cherished, would turn his back on him. He also knew that Peter, one of his closest friends, would deny him. In addition to this, he was aware that his time on earth was soon going to be over. He had cared for people, fed the hungry, healed the sick, spoken wisdom into people's lives, forgiven sins, but he had still been rejected. The emotional pain of this made Jesus weep. It absolutely and undoubtedly broke his heart.

That Sunday, after truly hearing the 'Hosanna' lyrics for the first time, I went to church and prayed out for God to break my heart with the things that break his. It's OK for me to get upset about poverty, injustice and challenging times. I wanted to be able to express my emotions in the correct way. I didn't end up crying that day, but it was the start of my journey into becoming more of an emotionally aware person, a person who genuinely cares about the things that God cares about. The truth is that God created us to have emotions. Whether male or female, it's OK to be happy, it's OK to be sad, it's OK to laugh and it's OK to cry.

Another passage I've found helpful is this: 'Do not be anxious about anything, but in everything by prayer and supplication with thanksgiving let your requests be made known to God. And the peace of God, which surpasses all understanding, will guard your hearts and your minds in Christ Jesus' (Philippians

4.6–7, ESV). I find this really comforting because it makes me feel that whatever the circumstance and whatever the weight on me emotionally, the peace of God is always there. Also, the fact I can pray for better days in times of trouble – and that God can hear me – makes this passage one of the most unforgettable in the Bible for me.

CHAPTER 5

FINDING FAITH

A few years ago, I went through a stage where I'd look up star-sign columns in various newspapers and read the section for Gemini, as my birthday is in June. There would always be something in them that I could get excited about. Here's what it said in a recent horoscope for Gemini:

> **Creation is your forte at the moment. You need to be spontaneous and focused on practical solutions at this moment in time. You can't be certain about the attitude behind someone's deeds, but this shouldn't stop you from working on your future plans.**

I now find astrology really funny because the advice always seems specific but is actually general enough to apply to anyone. I don't waste my time on them any more, but if we're honest with ourselves, the reason why people read this kind of stuff is because everyone is looking for a purpose in life, and the reason why we exist. Spiritual wellness is about finding that purpose and somehow managing to see our values and actions match up.

Complex magazine, an internationally recognised urban publication, asked me to write an article for their website on the part faith plays in urban music. I was incredibly excited about the prospect as I knew it was a fantastic opportunity and that thousands of people would read my work. As I started to develop some thoughts and put pen to paper, I realised that it was actually going to be just about the hardest thing I had ever written. When I'm writing for a Christian audience, the pressure is off because most readers or listeners will share some sort of common ground with me. When I'm writing for a mainstream audience, it's a bit trickier; people from different backgrounds, cultures and belief systems will come into contact with my work, and it's almost certain that not everyone will agree with my views. It's always a challenge to try and speak God's truth with love and grace. With that being said, I'm never one to shy away from a difficult task, so I started to write about how many urban musicians perceive God and the role that God can play in their lives.

One thing I've noticed is that when a musician wins an award of some sort, more often than not they're keen to thank God. They might say something like, 'Thank you, God, for blessing me with this gift. Without you this wouldn't have been possible.' For me that is encouraging to see but at the same time I would cast my mind back to some of the stand-out songs and lyrics from the artist. Very often their songs would celebrate the very things that God opposes, so it always made me wonder just how much they really valued God's input in their lives. This was a trend I witnessed beyond celebrity culture; it was also evident in the culture I was raised in.

I'll never forget the day one of my friends fleshed out a plan to steal a computer game from the local gaming shop. We were 13 years old and everyone else – including me – was too scared to even consider anything of the sort, but he didn't think twice. He went about his business and we saw him the next day grinning from ear to ear with the computer game in his hand. He was, of course, quick to entertain us with the tale of how it went down. After trying to make it sound as dramatic as possible, he ended with something like, 'It was close, but thank God I got away with it.' I remember instantly thinking, 'Why is he thanking God? Surely God didn't help him get away with stealing?!' Well, often this is the view that people can have. It's the belief that God helps us to fulfil the purpose we want for our lives, rather than God helping us to fulfil the purpose *he* wants for our lives.

I used to be guilty of viewing God as this kind of storybook character: this guy sitting way up there that I could occasionally pray to and ask for material stuff, and if he was in a good mood he'd answer. He was my personal genie and I had no need to speak to him otherwise. At least that's what I thought . . . until I had a skin condition that discoloured my face and I felt insecure. Then my favourite uncle died suddenly and I was overcome with sadness. Terrorists attacked London on 7 July 2005 and I felt fearful. In the middle of all these situations I realised that I needed to put my faith in something bigger than myself. It was great living life as my own king until it became clear that I didn't have control of the kingdom I lived in. There are lots of factors beyond my power and I need to put my hope in something unshakeable. Psalm 62.1–2 says, 'Truly my soul finds rest in God; my salvation comes from him. Truly he is my rock and my salvation: he is my fortress, I shall never be shaken' (NIV). For me, God has proved himself to be that unshakeable foundation.

Everyday Love

Rather than thinking of God as a genie, or a slot machine, a better vision is one of a loving parent. My mum really loves me. The ways in which she expresses that love leave me with no doubt in my mind that she wants the best for me. A great example of this was on my seventeenth birthday. I've been a big fan of cars pretty much all my life and I was really looking forward to being 17 because I could finally get my provisional licence and learn how to drive. Aware that a car of my own wasn't far off, I was on the AutoTrader website pretty much every day looking at different models of Mercedes and BMWs. I'm not sure why, because I couldn't even afford driving lessons at the time. I was so broke that I couldn't withdraw any notes from the cashpoint because my account balance was under £10. Have you ever gone into the bank and asked to take out £2.50 so you can buy chicken and chips? I have!

My parents weren't fans of handouts and they always taught me the value of hard work, so I didn't expect them to help buy me a car or contribute to any lessons. But to my surprise, for my birthday they bought me enough driving lessons to ensure that I'd pass my test. To you that may not be a big deal, but for me it was. I knew my parents didn't have loads of money and so I was shocked that they would do that for me. My mum later sat me down and said, 'Son, I didn't get you those driving lessons because I had money lying about or because I wanted to spoil you. I got you those lessons because some parts of London aren't safe at night, and I'd much rather you drive home than walk the streets or get on a bus or a train by yourself.' Looking back, I realise that my mum's intentions were to protect me because she loved me. She could have easily left me to sort out my driving lessons by myself, but she wanted the best for me.

Knowing that someone genuinely has your best interests at heart is a great feeling. With that being said, I don't just want my mother in my life when I need something, or when I'm in trouble; I want a supportive and loving figure like that to be involved in my life as much as possible. Also, from my mum's point of view, if I were to contact her only in times of need that would be very hurtful. The love she has shown me throughout my life is deserving of a consistent relationship between the two of us. We should think of God in the same way. We should want constant relationship with him every single day. His love for us is so deep that he doesn't just want to be there for us in the difficult times or on a Sunday at church, he wants to be part of our everyday lives.

True Success

Because we can't see God with our own eyes, we often fail to view him as a loved one with whom we can communicate in person. This may be why it's easier to forget about God and try and 'do life' without him. This is especially apparent when you see great things happening to people who don't seem to care about God. We could be forgiven for believing that if we do selfish things and get away with it, God must be OK with it. One thing I've struggled with is seeing evil or greedy people prosper. Why does God allow this to happen when there are people asking God for help to do the right things, but still waiting for answers?

I've come to realise that when self-centred, egotistical, greedy or evil people gain 'success', it isn't God blessing them at all. It's just them reaping the rewards of their wrong actions. For example, if I was to order a tap water at a restaurant, but then fill up my glass with Coke, the result would be me saving money because tap water is free but a Coke is not. God hasn't blessed my actions; rather it's just me trying to deceive people so that I can have an easier life. This may *sound* great, but deliberately doing wrong things in life means that one day we will face the consequences of our actions. If God were to stop our selfish and dishonest actions, he would be taking away our free will. Instead, he wants us to choose to do the right thing.

If that's true, then what is our reward for making the right choices in life? People who make evil choices seem to have all the money in the world, all the material possessions in the world, and all the power in the world – so what do the people who do right get? Well, the answer is true success in God's eyes.

White Lies

I've always told white lies. I started when I was quite young and carried on into my teenage years. I told lies when I wanted to impress people, or when I didn't want to disappoint them. I'd do things like tell my friends at school I had the latest computer game when in actual fact I had never even played it. I was also that friend who tells you they're ten minutes away when in actual fact they have only just got out of the shower. It didn't seem like I was doing anything wrong, but as I got older, the lies became more frequent and more unnecessary. I started to get found out by my friends and they began to stop trusting the words that came out of my mouth.

It may not seem like a big deal to you, but I really wanted to start being a man of my word. I recognised that for some reason, lying was a real temptation for me, and even though I was aware of it, I found it a struggle to ask for help. I didn't want to be branded a fake or for people to be disappointed in me, because I was well known as a role model.

In my experience, as soon as someone says they're a Christian, there can be an expectation for them to live a squeaky clean life. This was an issue I faced. Because of the kind of music I made, people started to put me on a pedestal and I felt a huge pressure to be perfect. I felt that if I made one mistake, everyone would be disappointed in me and think I was a hypocrite. But being perfect is an impossible task, and I found that out soon enough.

I once heard someone say, 'If you don't deal with the puddles, they'll turn into floods.' I was aware that if I didn't deal with the lying issue, it would turn into a bigger problem for me later on in life. I eventually decided that enough was enough. I chose to speak to a close friend and open up about it, and that was a helpful way of me overcoming my issue. That friend didn't judge me and recognised that I'm human and make mistakes like everybody else. I still make mistakes, of course, but for me the pressure is off because I'm comfortable with not being perfect.

God wants us to choose to do the right thing. It can be hard to change our actions or ways of thinking if they've been part of us for a long time, but we don't have to do it alone. I believe that God can help us become better people and he's shown us ways we can do this through giving us Jesus as the perfect example. I'll explore this in more detail later on.

CHAPTER 6

REFLECTION IN THE MIRROR

Taking pride in who God has made us is not something many Christians find easy, and I believe that's partly down to the messages we receive every day through the media. There are only so many 'get a body like Kim Kardashian' and 'abs like Cristiano Ronaldo' headlines I can take. I find it astonishing how much of an effect the media has on me subconsciously, though, be it through TV, magazines, websites or adverts. In early 2015, having recently proposed to my girlfriend, I decided to start buying the occasional wedding magazine with the hope that it would give me ideas on suits, décor and honeymoon destinations. As I looked through the pages in one particular magazine, it became apparent that 99 per cent of men who get married seemed to have a six-pack. I put the magazine down, walked up to my mirror and kind of lifted up my T-shirt to see how *my* six-pack was doing. All I can say is that it's a good thing the Bible says that faith the size of a mustard seed can move mountains because – in my reflection – I could see mountains of fat that needed to disappear! After a few half-hearted gym sessions, I realised that it was highly unlikely I'd be able to develop a sculpted torso in time for our honeymoon.

Looking back, I have to question where my heart was. Did I want to better my physical appearance to become healthier and fitter – or was I just envious of the finely toned, smiling models in the magazine? President Theodore Roosevelt once said that 'comparison is the thief of joy', and that was where my problem lay. After I proposed I was the happiest man on earth, and wedding planning was an exciting bonus. I felt extremely blessed and thankful for everything God was orchestrating in my life. But, as is the case with so many situations, I let comparison drift in and set up camp in my mind. As I flicked through those magazines, page by perfect page, I found myself lacking. That's when I was filled with envy, doubt, inferiority and dwindling self-confidence. That isn't what God wants for *any* of us, but it is the way the world can sometimes make us feel.

Please Mind the Gap

I grew up as quite a confident kid. I was never really self-conscious until I got to secondary school, when one of the class clowns shouted out across the room: 'The gap in your teeth is so big a sumo wrestler could fit through it.' To be totally honest it was quite funny at the time, but the gap-tooth jokes kept coming for the rest of my school life. I remember one occasion at the local train station when my friends and I had been waiting for a delayed train that was finally pulling up to the platform. As the doors opened the train announcer belted out, 'As you board this train, please mind the gap between the train and the platform. Please mind the gap.' Almost immediately, every single one of my friends looked

at me, paused for what seemed like an age, then proceeded
to laugh hysterically – implying that the train announcer was
referring to the gap in my teeth.

After that incident, I decided I'd had enough and that I
wanted to get braces. However, the truth is that I never really
wanted to. The gap *was* rather large, and a sumo wrestler
might have been able to fit through it, but that was neither
here nor there. What was important was that before I got to
secondary school I had never seen a problem with the gap in
my teeth. I had looked in the mirror hundreds of times and
been totally comfortable with the way I looked. The opinion of
people at school changed that.

Inside Out

In a world so focused on outward appearance, it's important
for me to remember that it's what's on the inside that
matters most. We need to stop viewing ourselves as faulty
mannequins and start realising that we were created
intentionally. Psalm 139.14 says, 'I praise you because I am
fearfully and wonderfully made; your works are wonderful,
I know that full well' (NIV). We're all created in the image of
God yet we are all unique. The same God that took care
in creating the stars in the sky took care in creating us. I think
it's absolutely fine to get braces to help straighten teeth, or

to change the colour of your hair, but we should never allow anyone to make us feel that there's something wrong with us. God doesn't make mistakes.

Another verse that encourages me when I don't do as well as I'd like to at the gym is 1 Timothy 4.8: 'Physical exercise has some value, but spiritual exercise is much more important, for it promises a reward in both this life and the next.'

I got braces for the same reason that I mainly work on my arms in the gym rather than my legs. I want the things that people are most likely to notice about me to look good, and I neglect the unseen. However, sometimes the unseen is the most important. Without my heart and my lungs my body can't function; just because you can't see them that doesn't mean they're not important. A perfect body is no good if my spirit isn't right. My confidence shouldn't be connected to my physical appearance – I should be confident because I belong to Jesus.

CHAPTER 7

THE QUEST FOR SUCCESS

Success is defined in the *Concise Oxford English Dictionary* as 'the accomplishment of an aim or purpose'. If an intern worked their way up to the top of a well-known company, they'd be called a success. However, if they got there by making false promises, exaggerating sales figures and lying to customers, would they still be considered successful? Sadly, in today's world they might be; but in God's eyes, maybe not.

On a Mission for Commission

I once had a job at one of the countless phone shops you find scattered around every town centre. I was a sales assistant and my job was simple: sell as many mobile phones, broadband packages and phone accessories as possible. After a few days working there, I realised that they took their targets very seriously. In the staff room there was a board with all our names written on it, alongside our targets. These targets were dependent on the number of hours we worked and were always quite challenging. I worked part-time, and every week I had to sell eight phone contracts, 12 pay-as-you-go sim cards, two broadband packages and £150 worth of accessories. If you met your targets, you would get paid a pretty mouth-watering commission at the end of the month, along with vouchers and other similar incentives.

My first few weeks were absolutely diabolical because I was way too honest. Someone would come in ready to buy a phone and I would say something like, 'You sure about that? I've heard it's not any good.' Unsurprisingly, that approach didn't get me many sales! The manager called me into his office and told me that I was possibly the worst sales rep he had ever employed. After that, I knew something had to change. Payslip or P45 terminating my employment? I know which one I'd rather receive. I left that meeting with an urge to sell with a vengeance. I started doing my research on the strong points of every mobile phone and ignored the weaknesses. I thought of ways I could sound appealing to new customers and I figured out I had this cheeky smile thing going on which people found friendly, so I used it as much as possible.

As all these factors combined I slowly turned into one of the most successful sellers in the store. The commission and free vouchers were coming in thick and fast and I gained a reputation among my colleagues as the man to learn from. After a while I had built up an untouchable status, which made me feel really good about myself.

Missing the Target

I remember one week that was particularly slow; there hadn't been many people in the shop, and I had one more contract phone to sell in order to reach my target. It was the last day of the week, with about 20 minutes left until closing time, when the sweetest lady walked through the door. She must have been in her fifties, her existing phone was beyond the point of repair and she was looking for a simple phone to make and receive calls only. She didn't surf the internet much and she hardly ever used texts. You may have heard the analogy of having the devil on one shoulder and an angel on the other. Well, the angel was telling me to give her exactly what she needed. At the time, it was probably a straightforward pay-as-you-go mobile, which was simple to use and would do everything she was looking for pretty easily. The battery lasts a long time on those phones too! The devil on my other shoulder reminded me of my targets for that week, and before I knew it I was trying to sell her a 64-gigabyte smartphone on a 12-month contract with 1,200 minutes and unlimited texts and data – not to mention the insurance, phone case and car charger. She wasn't tech savvy at all but she wasn't from the Stone Age either; I knew she would eventually learn how to use the complicated phone and its various features.

Ultimately, I had a choice to make: give her what she needed in the phone that would serve her best, or selfishly focus on meeting my targets by selling her one with tons of features that she would probably never use. Shamefully, I sold her the smartphone. It's the kind of thing people at my workplace did regularly without batting an eyelid, but for weeks afterwards I couldn't stop thinking about what I had done. I remember receiving my commission and feeling nothing. I had intentionally made the wrong decision out of greed, but when it came to reaping the rewards, I felt dissatisfied. After that uncomfortable experience, I decided to be a more honest seller and always do what was best for the customer. My sales started to dip, and feeling pressure from the manager to get results at any cost, it's no surprise that I didn't last very long at that place of work.

The Definition of Success

Growing up, I thought that success was being able to get a good job that paid incredibly well and also gave me plenty of holiday time so I could get in my expensive four-wheel drive car and go to France with my wife, our two kids and our trusty Labrador. Everything I earned was going to be used for *my* enjoyment and the things that *I* wanted to spend money on. I planned to save up as much as I could for my own personal gain. Charitable giving and helping out those in need never even crossed my mind.

Now I'm older and wiser, I know that having a great job or good position at work doesn't mean I'm successful, especially if I have acquired it in a dishonest and egotistical way. I'm not saying that we shouldn't strive to do the best we possibly can in our chosen occupation; I'm saying that we need to be doing so with the right motives.

Colossians 3.23–24 says: 'Whatever you do, work at it with all your heart, as working for the Lord, not for human masters, since you know that you will receive an inheritance from the Lord as a reward. It is the Lord Christ you are serving' (NIV). That not only encourages me to be less greedy, it encourages me to be less lazy. Being sluggish and not working at all can be equally as damaging as being greedy. I think a good way to measure success is to look at what you've done with what God has given you, and at the kind of person that journey is making you become.

What's in Your Hands?

One of my favourite stories in the Bible is the Parable of the Talents. I like it because it shows that God has given everyone something. You may not have a voice like Adele's, a business brain like Bill Gates's, or feet like Neymar's, but you've got something. This parable reminds me that there is no excuse for not having a work ethic. We must all strive to do the best we can with what God has placed in us. Matthew 25.14–29 sets the scene:

The Parable of the Talents

For it will be like a man going on a journey, who called his servants and entrusted to them his property. To one he gave five talents, to another two, to another one, to each according to his ability. Then he went away. He who had received the five talents went at once and traded with them, and he made five talents more. So also he who had the two talents made two talents more. But he who had received the one talent went and dug in the ground and hid his master's money.

Now after a long time the master of those servants came and settled accounts with them. And he who had received the five talents came forward, bringing five talents more, saying, 'Master, you delivered to me five talents; here I have made five talents more.'

His master said to him, 'Well done, good and faithful servant. You have been faithful over a little; I will set you over much. Enter into the joy of your master.'

And he also who had the two talents came forward, saying, 'Master, you delivered to me two talents; here I have made two talents more.'

His master said to him, 'Well done, good and faithful servant. You have been faithful over a little; I will set you over much. Enter into the joy of your master.'

He also who had received the one talent came forward, saying, 'Master, I knew you to be a hard man, reaping where you did not sow, and gathering where you scattered no seed, so I was afraid, and I went and hid your talent in the ground. Here you have what is yours.'

But his master answered him, 'You wicked and slothful servant! You knew that I reap where I have not sown and gather where I scattered no seed? Then you ought to have invested my money with the bankers, and at my coming I should have received what was my own with interest.

So take the talent from him and give it to him who has the ten talents. For to everyone who has will more be given, and he will have an abundance. But from the one who has not, even what he has will be taken away.' (ESV)

God doesn't want us to live safe, comfortable lives. Our goal shouldn't be to die old, it should be to die empty. Erma Bombeck puts it beautifully: 'When I stand before God at the end of my life, I would hope that I would not have a single bit of talent left, and could say, "I used everything you gave me".'

Shifting Shadows

Place your hand over your heart right now. Go on, I'm waiting! If you can feel your heart beating, that's called purpose. If you can't, you *might* want to call an ambulance.

Seriously, though, we are alive not by chance, but because God has a specific plan for each of our lives here on earth. I strongly believe that he has gifted every single one of us with unique abilities and strengths. Our talent is God's gift to us and what we do with it is our gift back. He's not going to change his mind either. It's not like one day he'll think, 'Actually, I'm going to take the talent away.' The world we live in might offer us things and then decide to take them back, but that's not how God works. He doesn't change with the wind. James 1.17 says, 'Every good and perfect gift is from above, coming down from the Father of the heavenly lights, who does not change like shifting shadows' (NIV).

Sometimes we can easily overlook the things that God has given us because they don't slap us right in the face. I never wanted to be a rapper; in fact, I didn't know what I wanted to do. I enjoyed things like music and football but I never really saw myself as being particularly skilled in those fields. I actually started off rapping as a joke in the playground at school. We would compete with each other and whoever said the most offensive thing about their opponent's mother

would win. Back then I was very good at saying not very
nice things so I would often win the rap battles. Even after
numerous victories, I still didn't realise that there was a gift
hiding somewhere inside of me – even if I was using it in the
wrong way. Eventually, I opened my eyes and was able to see
that I had something special that God had given me.

Finding Your Drive

But what about you? Do you know what God has put inside of
you? If you do, then that's great – start using it! If you don't,
here are a few clues as to how to find that out.

1 What Do You Really Enjoy?

Your gift or talent is always going to be something you
actually *enjoy*. God wants you to make the most of life and
have fun while doing it. John 10.10 says, 'The thief comes
only to steal and kill and destroy; I have come that they may
have life, and have it to the full' (NIV). What do you enjoy
doing? What takes up most of your spare time?

2 What Are You Naturally Gifted At?

If I were to ask who the best footballer in the world is, the
responses might point me towards Cristiano Ronaldo or Lionel
Messi. Personally, as a West Ham fan, I'd go for Dimitri Payet,
but that's another story for another day. All you have to do

is watch Ronaldo or Messi play to realise that you could train every single minute of every single day, and never reach their level of greatness. I imagine they both work incredibly hard, but there's no doubt that they are naturally gifted at what they do. Is there anything you naturally excel at? Is there something you can do with half the effort of your friends but double the skill?

3 What Concerns You?

When I became a Christian, it worried me that there wasn't enough positive and inspirational rap music for me to listen to. Nine out of ten rap songs were about taking or selling drugs, having promiscuous sex and obtaining as much money as possible. It disturbed me so much that I decided to be the answer to my problem, by recording alternative music with a more uplifting message. That's how my career started. 1 Peter 4.10 says this: 'As each has received a gift, use it to serve one another, as good stewards of God's varied grace' (ESV). Find out whether there are ways in which you can impact people and serve them. What annoys you? What issue are you super passionate about? Homelessness? Human trafficking? Police brutality? Bullying? You could possess the gift to be part of the change you want to see.

The answers to the questions above are likely to lead you into your area of interest and your God-given purpose. No matter your age, background or situation, it's never too late to start taking steps into using what God has given you.

CHAPTER 8

PURPOSE AND PASSION

In the previous chapters I explained some ways in which I believe we can be enabled to find satisfaction, peace and hope in this world. But one of the age-old questions about life remains: why? Why are we here and what is our purpose? This isn't a book that professes to have all the answers to the difficult questions in life; I'm just as baffled as the next person. What this book *is*, though, is a compass to point us in the direction of the one who *does* know all the answers.

I take the same approach with my music. Recently I performed at a festival in the east of England with my DJ, JimmyJames. There were around 600 people there and we all had the time of our lives. The staging, lighting and sound system helped to create a great vibe and the energy in the room was incredible. During my performance I noticed a young boy around the age of 13 who really stood out. A number of people knew some of the words to the songs, and there were probably a few there who had never heard of me before, but this chap knew every single word to every single track. I even held the microphone out to him at one point because he was performing my music better than I was! As I finished my sweaty performance, Jimmy and I grabbed a couple of towels and strolled over to the merchandise stand to sign some CDs. After about 20 minutes, a lady came over to me and said, 'There was a boy in the front row. He's a big fan and your music has really helped him. Here's a letter. Please read it when you can.'

I immediately knew which boy she was talking about. I expressed my gratitude, folded up the letter and put it into my pocket. I finished the signing session, packed down my gear and got in my car ahead of the three-hour drive back to London. I took out the letter and slouched back in my seat to read it.

Hi Guvna B!

Just to say God working through you has truly saved my son. His dad was an alcoholic and so that caused him to struggle at school. He saw and heard many things that a kid really shouldn't. He is now dealing with being a lad with Autistic Spectrum Disorder. He hates himself a lot of the time. He puts his earphones on in his room and all he does is rap and remember all your tunes. It takes him to a great place away from it all and gives him hope.

Thank you.

It was truly humbling to read this letter, and a gentle reminder that maybe, just maybe, the reason for why we are here is bigger than ourselves. I've received several letters over the last decade detailing how my music has helped people overcome addiction, suicidal thoughts, insecurity, depression and so much more. When I started music I'd be lying if I said that was my aim. All I wanted to do was use my God-given gift to the best of my ability. Through doing that, I've been continually reminded that our purpose here on earth is so much bigger than ourselves.

Breaking the Norm

My twenty-fifth birthday was a huge wake-up call for me. Every birthday before that had been met with excitement and anticipation, but the morning I turned 25 I felt quite low and empty. I had a great family and really good friends, my music career was going well, and I had recently met Emma, the girl I'd marry one year later. On the outside looking in, most would say that I wasn't doing badly – but on the inside I felt dull.

My parents worked remarkably hard in order to move over to the UK from Ghana and set up a better life for me and my younger brother Joel, and I am incredibly proud of what they've managed to achieve. I was brought up with the mantra that 'anything is possible if you work hard enough', but this was often in relation to the targets my parents had programmed into my mind. These targets were based on the usual expectations within African culture: work hard, so that you get good exam results, so that you can get a good job, so that you can get a mortgage, and have some kids, who can then repeat the cycle.

I didn't get the first part of that cycle right; I got it horribly wrong. I didn't work hard in school, which led to me achieving only five GCSEs, and both my teachers and I knew I was capable of so much more. While my GCSE results weren't anything to shout about, my mum showed her kindness by going easy on me because I *somehow* still managed to get into college. I repaid her kindness by getting two Es and two Us in my first year of college. She wasn't so compassionate that time!

Looking back, I'm still really disappointed in myself for getting those grades, but knowing my friend's GCSE results spelt the word DUDE makes me feel better! Seriously though, I managed, miraculously, to redo a couple of exams, get better grades, and eventually I went on to graduate from the University of Hertfordshire.

So there I was on my birthday with a degree, a successful career and a girlfriend who I strongly believed would become my wife. Yet as the birthday texts rolled in, I remember lying in my bed thinking: 'If this is what life is all about, why do I feel so dull? Surely there's more to life than good grades, starting a family, buying a house, paying bills and then dying?' Those thoughts would act as fuel on the journey to me finding out my true purpose. I prayed, and while I can't remember the prayer word for word, it was along these lines. It may be relevant to you too:

Lord, I don't know why I'm here but I know that I'm
alive for a reason. I don't want to succumb to living a
'normal' life and following the same patterns that have
been cemented for generations. I want to live a radical,
adventurous, exciting, risky and faith-filled life, walking
the path that you have set out for me. Help me to find my
purpose, and dream dreams and see visions so big that
they're impossible to achieve without your help. Amen.

After I prayed that prayer, I felt a sense of liberation and
peace. It made me feel confident and fearless. There's
something about trusting God to work in your life and
knowing that he will protect you. It makes it easier to take
risks and break the norms. That prayer was just the beginning,
though. Words don't mean much if you're not willing to live
them out.

All In

I've never been the strongest reader and I've struggled to
read the Bible on many occasions. It doesn't help that the
first Bible I was given was the confusingly ancient King James
version. I was left more muddled than the Roman soldiers on
the third day, faced with an empty tomb. With that being said,
when I decided to take my faith seriously, I didn't want to be a
wishy-washy Christian who just picked out the most enjoyable

bits of Scripture. I wanted to fully commit to everything that came with it, the easy stuff and the more challenging stuff too. I wouldn't be a very good friend if I always borrowed money from my mates but never paid them back. In the same way, I wouldn't be a very good Christian if I accepted all the blessings God gives me, without doing the work needed on my side to get to know him. For that very reason, I made a real effort to try and read the Bible. I found two versions that I really liked and stuck to those: the New International Version along with *The Message*. I also started to listen to an audio version of the Bible, which really suited me as a way to digest the Scriptures. Through making that concerted effort, the words on the pages started to jump out at me and I began to relate to them, but – most importantly – I started to realise why I'm here. Finding out my purpose, through verses such as the two below, would go on to shape the way I've been living my life ever since.

'For in him all things were created: things in heaven and on earth, visible and invisible, whether thrones or powers or rulers or authorities; all things have been created through him and for him' (Colossians 1.16, NIV). When I first read this verse, I thought God was a bit of a control freak to be honest. All things in this world were created by him and for him. Isn't that a bit selfish? Shouldn't the purpose of our lives be to do whatever *we* want? That thought process lingered in my head for a while but then I came across another verse shortly after.

'You are worthy, our Lord and God, to receive glory and
honour and power, for you created all things, and by your will
they were created and have their being' (Revelation 4.11, NIV).
The word 'worthy' really stuck out for me. It means to have
qualities that deserve a specific action. Without God, I can't
exist. He not only created me, he created everything I see.
He is worthy of my praise because he has proved that he has
insurmountable qualities, and is the only being in the universe
fully deserving of glory. I strongly believe that we're all
designed to worship something. What are you worshipping?
Some may say that worship is a big word to use but I believe
it's true. We human beings have something inside us that
inspires zealous dedication to certain things, from sports
teams to famous faces. All you need to do to verify that
statement is speak to a Justin Bieber fan.

Forever Blowing Bubbles

I have my own obsessions and one of them carries three
of the most important words you will ever hear: West Ham
United. In 2005 I was at the Millennium Stadium to watch a
Championship play-off final between West Ham and Preston
North End. As an avid West Ham fan I was nervous and
excited all at once. The game was tense and opportunities
were few and far between. Whoever won the game would
be promoted to the Premier League, so there was a lot

on the line. After a fairly non-eventful first half, the second started much brighter for West Ham, and in the fifty-seventh minute Bobby Zamora popped up in the opposition's box, and volleyed home the only goal of the game: the goal that would help West Ham clinch promotion to the Premier League.

The absolute pandemonium that followed was incredible. It was one of the best atmospheres I have ever been a part of. I was hugging people I had never met before in jubilation. We marched the streets blowing bubbles and singing songs for hours on end. West Ham flags were being waved as high as the sky and people from different backgrounds were unified through their love for football.

That memory stays with me because after reading the verse in Revelation 4.11, I started to think about the things that I praise and the things I'm most passionate about. I thought about how passionate I am when I go to a home match and sing our anthem 'Forever Blowing Bubbles', but how flat I can be in church when I'm singing songs to Jesus. I felt a strong conviction to give my praise primarily to God because he is worthy of it. I naively thought that God wanted glory because he was self-centred and fame-hungry. The reality is that God doesn't need our affirmation, but we need him. Glorifying God opens up the door to many things that benefit us and that's because he loves us.

It's OK to enjoy the things that make us happy, and to be a fan of something, but it needs to be with the realisation that we're never going to find true fulfilment in those things. We can only find purpose in the One who created us.

CHAPTER 9

THE TRUE EXAMPLE

My dad is my kind of guy. I remember one time when my mum and my younger brother went away to Spain for a week and my dad and I were looking forward to spending some quality time together and taking part in some exciting activities. Various things may pop into your mind. Maybe some classic father-and-son bonding fun like fishing, camping or biking. Well, we did nothing of the sort. Our idea of father-and-son time was sitting on the sofa with our feet up, watching *Match of the Day* while eating a Chinese takeaway. That pattern continued for the whole of the week. We just chilled, ate food and watched sports. It was our way and I loved it.

I consider myself very fortunate to have grown up with my dad. He's a generous, loving and hard-working man who has always set a great example for my brother Joel and me. Though my family have faced testing times, he has stuck around through them all and always remained optimistic. Growing up with him as my male role model enabled me to take on some of his characteristics, such as perseverance, humility and gentleness. I wouldn't be exaggerating, though, if I said that growing up with a father figure was a reality for about only a quarter of my friends on the council estate where I grew up. Most of the local kids either had dads who weren't around or their father–son relationships were fractured. Some had never even met their biological fathers. When we were younger, my friends could not have known how the experience of growing up without a father figure would affect them. Decades later, some still feel the effects of being abandoned by their dads.

My heart first broke for fatherlessness when I started mentoring students and delivering workshops in schools. Travelling up and down the country supporting teenagers in schools is something I've been doing for several years. Soon after I started the role, it became apparent that the majority of those students who were struggling to reach their full potential came from homes without a father figure to guide them. It's something I really empathised with and I wished there was something I could do to make their situations better. Through reading the Bible and discovering my purpose, I found an interesting revelation.

The Father's Love

Our purpose is to please God and that should be our primary goal as recipients of his love and grace. However, the great thing is that God cares for us so much that there's a huge amount of blessing in it for us too. One of the most humbling of those is that he is a father to all, including the fatherless. Our purpose in life is to never feel abandoned, but feel a sense of belonging to God – the Father who loves us unconditionally has provided us with every blessing, and will never leave us.

This realisation became a source of comfort for some of the young people I mentored, and also for my friends without fathers. Even for me, though I had a dad who was around, it was added encouragement. Knowing I had a heavenly Father helped me to understand why I was created and gave me courage to press on in life. It was as if I had become a Christian all over again and I was itching to make an impact in the world. The trouble was that I had an enormous amount of passion but no clue about how to use it – a bit like those fire and brimstone preachers you find on teetering pedestals in busy London shopping districts.

I remember one particular occasion a few years ago when I was walking up Oxford Street with a friend who wasn't a Christian. As we got closer to the traffic lights, we could hear one of the most disliked voices in London getting louder and louder. 'Turn or burn! Hell is around the corner!' the street preacher belted through his megaphone. I felt absolutely gutted. This isn't how I wanted my friend to view Christianity. It's not an uncompassionate, insensitive, persecuting religion. In my experience, street preachers only tend to concentrate on the 'bad news' of God's message, and in a sensationalist way, when the word 'gospel', in fact, means 'good news'. Telling people they're going to hell isn't good news, that's pretty bad news! Good news would be to display God's love and share his truth in a considerate way.

Highlighting one side of the story but excluding the other isn't telling the whole truth. The whole truth is normally a combination of both. Yes, the bad news is that we're imperfect people in need of saving because we can't protect ourselves from the consequences of our wrongdoings. But the good news is that Jesus was the sacrifice for our mistakes and, if we accept that, we can move forward in our lives without fear.

So with my newfound understanding of the extent of God's love, how was I to share this game-changing news in the right way? How could I live a life that was pleasing to God, and what did that even mean? Fortunately for me, it wasn't an equation I'd have to solve by myself. Two thousand years ago, someone walked this earth and pleased God in the perfect way. I had a faultless role model to look at – an inspiring example to learn from. His name was Jesus.

Jesus Stands Tall When We Come Up Short

Luke 19.10 says that Jesus came 'to seek and to save the lost'. He was on a mission, he knew that this mission would glorify God, and he never strayed from that assignment. How did he engage with the culture around him? How did he carry out his mission in a loving way? Well, let's take a look at an example.

Zacchaeus the Tax Collector

Jesus entered Jericho and was passing through. A man was there by the name of Zacchaeus; he was a chief tax collector and was wealthy. He wanted to see who Jesus was, but because he was short he could not see over the crowd. So he ran ahead and climbed a sycamore-fig tree to see him, since Jesus was coming that way.

When Jesus reached the spot, he looked up and said to him, 'Zacchaeus, come down immediately. I must stay at your house today.' So he came down at once and welcomed him gladly.

All the people saw this and began to mutter, 'He has gone to be the guest of a sinner.'

But Zacchaeus stood up and said to the Lord, 'Look, Lord! Here and now I give half of my possessions to the poor, and if I have cheated anybody out of anything, I will pay back four times the amount.'

Jesus said to him, 'Today salvation has come to this house, because this man, too, is a son of Abraham. For the Son of Man came to seek and to save the lost.' (Luke 19.1–10, NIV)

This has to be one of my favourite stories from the Bible. To truly appreciate it you need to understand what kind of person Zacchaeus was. He made money by profiting from extremely poor people, taking from the less fortunate to make himself richer. In those days, most tax collectors were dishonest and charged citizens way beyond what they owed. Imagine if I was a wealthy man living in an impoverished area in a developing country. The people who lived in this area struggled to afford food or a roof over their heads. Imagine if I decided to take the little that these people had in order to make myself even richer. What Zacchaeus was doing was equally as bad.

Most people dislike tax collectors who do their jobs correctly and fairly, so imagine the hatred people must have had for Zacchaeus. The passage says that Zacchaeus was trying to catch a sight of Jesus but he couldn't see through the crowd because he was so small. Whenever I'm at a concert and someone shorter than me can't see, I just let them stand in front of me, because I'll still be able to see. That didn't happen on this occasion; because people disliked Zacchaeus so much, they refused to let him through. As we can see from the passage, Zacchaeus decided to climb up a tree and Jesus spotted him as he was walking by. Jesus told him to come down, as he wanted to have dinner at Zacchaeus' house. This last section is the part that astounds me.

Talk of the Town

Jericho was one of the most powerful cities at the time, so it could be likened to London. Jesus had built up quite a reputation for himself, and at this point he was a fully fledged celebrity. Imagine Adele walking through Piccadilly Circus. It would have been somewhere around that level of excitement. The difference is, Adele would probably be meeting someone really important, like another celebrity – a movie star, an MP, the Queen . . . who knows? She would most certainly not be seen going into the house of one of the most hated men in the city. The damage it could do to her brand would be catastrophic. What would people think?

The townsfolk were already gossiping about Jesus and questioning his actions, but Jesus wasn't focused on that. He was focused on building a relationship with Zacchaeus so that he could make an impact on his life for the better. Jesus didn't need Zacchaeus to change before he spoke to him or sat down to eat with him. He accepted Zacchaeus even before Zacchaeus was ready to change. For me, this is one of the best aspects of Christianity. Rather than God saying that we need to change before we can be accepted by him, the Bible tells us that God has already accepted us, and this acceptance leads us to want to change for the better. We can see this in the extract from Luke's Gospel. Jesus' approach worked and Zacchaeus was so affected by his unconditional love that he decided to pay back the money he had taken four times over.

Camera Flash

In 2010 I won my first MOBO Award for Best Gospel Artist. It was an exciting night for me as it was my first ever nationally recognised nomination and I knew that a huge proportion of the UK would be watching the ceremony on TV. While I was getting ready at the hotel for the event at the ECHO Arena in Liverpool, my manager at the time informed me that all the nominees had to arrive an hour before the show to walk the red carpet and speak to the press. Straight away I started thinking about all the interviews I would be doing with different publications and TV stations, and I even walked up to the mirror a few times practising poses for the paparazzi. During the short car ride I remember getting more and more nervous, and the butterflies were fluttering madly as we pulled up to the VIP entrance of the arena. We were fifth in a queue of cars, and I peered out to see who I could spot as celebrities stepped out of each vehicle ahead of us to process along the red carpet.

Car doors opened, and the fans who had been queuing for hours started screaming and waving their homemade

banners. JLS got out of the first car, followed by Jessie J
in the second, Emeli Sandé in the third, and Tinie Tempah up
next. All I could see were camera flashes and fans throwing
their hands out trying to get the attention of the stars on the
red carpet. Our driver said, 'Right, you're up next. Here we
go.' I did one last check in the mirror and gave the driver
the nod to open the door for me. As I stepped out on to the
red carpet, in front of hundreds of MOBO fans, about three
people screamed. They were half-hearted screams at that,
and I'm pretty sure they only did it because they thought
I was Dizzee Rascal. I then proceeded to go on one of the
most embarrassing and un-VIP walks of my life. One solitary
girl screamed at me and handed me a piece of paper to sign,
although I'm 99 per cent certain it was just in case she found
out later on I was someone famous. I then strolled past MTV,
BBC Radio 1Xtra and Sky News, to name a few, but none of
the press wanted to chat. For most of them I was their tea
break. It felt like the longest red carpet in history.

Just before the VIP section, I had to walk past the area where
the paparazzi were gathered to take pictures. Tinie Tempah
was just in front of me, and all I could hear were yells of
'Tinie, look at me! Tinie, over here! Tinie, one more picture!'
Then it was my turn. I walked up to the paparazzi and – you
guessed it – no one was interested. Instead of 'Guvna, look at
me! Guvna, over here! Guvna, one more picture!', it was,
'Who's that?' One photographer took my picture but I think it

was because he felt sorry for me. Whoever that photographer was, if you're reading this, thanks, mate.

After I left the red carpet, I headed into the VIP section full of celebrities, some of whom I grew up listening to. I was there as a nominee, but I was also a fan. The personalities and music artists gathered there included The Jackson 5 (who were The Jackson 4 then, as Michael Jackson had sadly passed away a few months before). Even though I had the opportunity to approach them, I found it very difficult to pluck up the courage. I didn't want to seem weird or like a crazed fan, and I definitely didn't want them to find me annoying. A lot of people were already immersed in conversations and some of them looked like they weren't in the mood to talk.

One thing that strikes me about Jesus is that sometimes he approached people, like he did with Zacchaeus, but on other occasions he waited for people to approach him. Not only that, but whenever they did come to him he was always open to interacting with them. It was totally counter-cultural; celebrities aren't always open to that interaction, and Jesus was a celebrity. He never intended to be one, and that wasn't his goal, but when you look at how many people followed him constantly when he walked the earth, he would have been considered a superstar in today's world. I find it incredible that he was so easily approachable. He came across as welcoming, friendly and open to talking to people no matter who they were. This is something I try to replicate. Not because I think I'm a superstar in today's world, but because I'm inspired by the example of Jesus. I make an effort to say hello to security guards, ask waitresses how they're doing, and to tell the postman to have a good day. Too many relationships these days are transactional. 'I'll do this for you if you do this for me' or 'I'll scratch your back if you scratch mine.' I've found it quite fulfilling to spread love and go the extra mile for people without expecting anything in return.

The Bleeding Woman

Another example of Jesus' friendliness is the story of the bleeding woman. I love this story as it shows that even with a huge number of followers and excitement all around him, Jesus is so aware of what's happening. In the middle of a crowd of people, Jesus is always looking out for each individual. Jesus didn't have all the time in the world here, with a crowd of people following his every step. Even so, he refused to be rushed and stood there while the woman explained why she touched his garments. Mark sets the scene in chapter 5.

A large crowd followed and pressed round him. And a woman was there who had been subject to bleeding for twelve years. She had suffered a great deal under the care

of many doctors and had spent all she had, yet instead
of getting better she grew worse. When she heard about
Jesus, she came up behind him in the crowd and touched his
cloak, because she thought, 'If I just touch his clothes, I will
be healed.' Immediately her bleeding stopped and she felt in
her body that she was freed from her suffering.

At once Jesus realised that power had gone out from him.
He turned round in the crowd and asked, 'Who touched
my clothes?'

'You see the people crowding against you,' his disciples
answered, 'and yet you can ask, "Who touched me?"'

But Jesus kept looking around to see who had done it. Then
the woman, knowing what had happened to her, came and fell
at his feet and, trembling with fear, told him the whole truth.
He said to her, 'Daughter, your faith has healed you. Go in
peace and be freed from your suffering.' (Mark 5.24–34, NIV)

Touching someone's clothes without permission in a public
place isn't a normal thing to do. If that happened to me on a
busy London street, I'd probably assume someone was trying
to steal my phone. Anyone trying to touch a celebrity would
probably get rugby-tackled to the ground by a security guard.
Jesus is different. He didn't think it was weird and he didn't
get offended. He saw the woman's heart and all he wanted

to do was help. We read that he felt the power had gone out from him. Jesus' loss was someone else's gain. And he tells the woman: 'Daughter, your faith has healed you. Go in peace and be freed from your suffering.' Many would have seen that situation as an inconvenience, but Jesus saw it as an opportunity to set someone free.

Humble Heroes

One of the most memorable experiences in my life came as a result of someone being willing to give some of their power and influence away and share what they had, just as Jesus does in the passage above.

I had been booked to play a concert at the youth venue of one of the biggest annual Christian events in Europe. I was to perform during the day and Matt Redman happened to be playing the main arena that evening. In case you haven't heard of Matt Redman, he's one of the most well-known Christian artists of our generation. He was the soundtrack to my life growing up, along with Kirk Franklin and Mary Mary, and other rappers from the 1990s and early millennium like Eminem, Jay Z, Nas and 50 Cent.

After my performance in the day, I found a text message on my phone from one of the singers in Matt Redman's band, who was a good friend of mine. He asked me to join them at the main arena, as Matt wanted to have a word with me.

I walked over and as soon as I saw Matt, he hit me with it. 'Hey, mate, thanks for coming over. Really love what you do and I was wondering whether you'd be up for joining us on stage tonight. I think the energy would be great.' I played it cool but in my head I was doing somersaults. I'd just been asked to go on stage at the iconic O2 Arena with one of my musical inspirations! Of course I accepted the offer, and had the most incredible night inspiring and encouraging thousands of people through the music.

In the grand scheme of things, Matt didn't need me to perform with him that night. He's a Grammy award-winning artist who is more than capable of playing music without the help of a Z-list rapper from east London. I think Matt had me on stage that evening because he genuinely loves sharing what he has and investing in people regardless of their achievements or popularity.

That night, and on many occasions since, I've been inspired by the humility of some of my greatest musical heroes. When they could boast about so much, they instead choose to look at how they can share their knowledge and serve others. My mother always told me that talent will only get you so far, but character will keep you there, and it's clear to see why some of the artists I've worked with have enjoyed great success and longevity. C. S. Lewis said, 'True humility isn't thinking less of yourself; it is thinking of yourself less.' I think our world would be a better place if we all tried to live by these words.

CHAPTER 10

IMPACTING CULTURE

In today's culture we're used to looking up to celebrities because of their talent or good looks or because we aspire to be like them. For me, Jesus' characteristics are inspiring and a great representation of how to live life and make a difference. It's his example that I want to follow and set my course by. As I read about Jesus, three main points stand out to me concerning the impact he had on culture.

1 Jesus knew what he stood for.
2 Jesus was a people's person.
3 Jesus didn't have a comfort zone.

Jesus was patient, loving and kind and he displayed those characteristics wherever he went. He spoke to people in the workplace and in their homes. He didn't need a special environment or control over the circumstances to share love and hope. He asked questions and connected with people's thoughts and feelings. He rarely forced or pressed people to turn their lives around instantly; instead he understood that often people need time to think and process the wisdom he so easily shared.

Sometimes I wonder whether Jesus would find it harder to walk the earth today than he did 2,000 years ago. While I'll never know the answer to that question, my imagination tends to run wild. He would certainly face different challenges in our modern culture. Would he need to conjure up a vegan option at the feeding of the 5,000? Would he be late to the Sermon on the Mount because his Uber got stuck in traffic? How viral would the video go if someone Snapchatted him walking on water? Would Peter follow him back on Instagram? Who knows.

What I *do* know is that in Hebrews we read that Jesus Christ is the same yesterday, today and for ever. That gives me confidence that even though times have changed drastically, his principles and passions remain the same. I have no doubt that if he was alive in human form on earth today, he'd still have an impact on this ever-changing world with his never-changing love.

I once heard a friend say, 'You can't fight today's battles with yesterday's tools.' In a practical sense I'd agree with that statement. If I released my next album on cassette rather than on iTunes, it would probably sell next to no copies. If I put music videos on VCR instead of YouTube, not many people would have the chance to see them. With that being said, I believe that you *can* fight today's battles with yesterday's tools – instruments that have stood the test of time. Faith, love, peace, hope and forgiveness are tools that will always help us greatly in the trials of the present day. Jesus gave his life so that we could live ours, and he not only told us how to live, he showed us too. He lived a perfect life on earth. Alone, this is impossible for us, but with God's help we can live a life inspired by Jesus. But how best can we follow his example? Let's take a look at the three main points mentioned above about the impact Jesus had on culture. If we can apply these same principles to our lives, the hope is that we too can influence our own culture and make this world a better place.

Jesus Knew What He Stood For

As a Christian who makes music, I'm always drawn to opportunities where I can perform outside of the Church. I love playing to Christians, and the great thing about that is that they already know about Jesus and the benefits of committing our lives to him. When I perform to non-believers in a more mainstream or urban audience, I get this satisfying feeling that I'm bringing God's light into a dark place. Christians can find themselves in dark places too, but being in a dark place and knowing there is a light is different from being in a dark place without any knowledge of hope. There are people who still think music made by Christians is one-dimensional, fitting into the categories of hymns and traditional worship songs. Though I am fond of those styles of songs, I love breaking down stereotypes and showing people the various ways in which God can use people artistically. However, even though I find non-Christian gigs exciting, they do come with their challenges.

After around three years of taking music seriously, the opportunity came up to take part in a community-based initiative, where a youth organisation put on a concert for young people in the local area. To attract as many individuals as possible, a few high-profile urban artists were to appear, all with quite a following. I was one of the lesser-known acts on the line-up, but I still got a great response from the audience. The more popular acts followed and the audience went crazy for them. Even though I didn't agree with a lot of the content those acts shared in their music, I respected their talent and artistry. I could probably learn a thing or two from them and I had a heart to get to know them better in the hope that I could share some positivity and perhaps they could learn from me too.

The opportunity arose after the show when one of the popular acts was chilling out backstage with some of his mates. They were relatively friendly and a few of them had caught a few minutes of my performance and enjoyed it. The conversation flowed pretty easily between us and we spoke about music and our future plans. The conversation had settled into general chit-chat when a member of their entourage brought in some marijuana. Having been raised in inner-city London, I was used to people smoking weed, but it was something I had never dabbled in myself. The guy with the weed made his way around the room passing some to everyone and eventually he got to me. That moment in and of itself happened pretty quickly, but whenever I reminisce I'm reminded of the subconscious thoughts that went through my mind in those few seconds. 'They must already think I'm weird because I'm a Christian; they'll be even more judgemental if I turn this down. They're cool guys, a bit of weed won't do any harm. It's going to be a pretty awkward situation if I say no.'

It's easy to know what you stand for when you're around like-minded people; it's a lot harder when you're with people who don't care about the standards you have set for yourself. I politely declined the drugs, and the artist was intrigued enough to ask why: 'You don't smoke weed, and I realised while watching you earlier that your lyrics are quite positive. Are you religious?' In responding, I was able to open up about what I stand for. I was given the opportunity to explain that I'm not religious in the sense of believing in following a set of rules and regulations just for the sake of it. Instead, I'm a man of faith and becoming a Christian has made me feel that God is always looking after me. That gives me all the relief and the buzz I need so I've never really felt that weed was for me. I also mentioned how my music is an expression of my world, and being a Christian shapes my world view, so it's natural for my lyrics to be positive. They had huge respect for what I shared and asked a lot of questions, and great conversation followed. Being true to myself rather than compromising in that situation was the right thing to do and I'm confident I left a positive impact with those in that room.

A wise man once said that if you don't stand for something, you'll fall for anything. Jesus came to give life and life to the full. He was on a mission to bring a light into dark places and he had an impact on culture because he was focused on his mission. We can do the same. What do you stand for?

Jesus Was a People's Person

If you know my music or if you follow me on social media, you will know that my catchphrase is 'Allo, mate'. In all honesty, it came about at the start of my music career in a really random way when I was asked to contribute a rap on a tune called 'Bun da Gun'. Please don't YouTube the song because I sound like a seven-year-old girl. Anyway, the song was about the plight of those affected by gun violence in the UK and it encouraged people to stop playing around with dangerous firearms. There were a few artists on the track, and my verse started off as follows:

> 'Allo, mate, and it's Guvna B
> And I told you before to put the guns down

I had moved from east London to Essex a couple of years earlier, and I had somehow managed to adopt a cockney accent, so my verse on that song sounded really distinctive. From the moment it was released, every time someone saw me they'd say, 'Allo, mate!' It was clearly a memorable phrase and one that people associated with me; I carried on mentioning it in my lyrics and it eventually evolved into a merchandise line. It was never meant to have a profound, underlying meaning but I found that it took that route after a trip to New York with my friend – and fellow rapper – Nick Brewer.

We had finished college and were both soon to go off to different universities, so we decided to go away on a boys' holiday to the Big Apple. As soon as we stepped off the plane into scorching heat we could already tell the difference between New York and London. It was hot for more than two days at a time for a start. One thing that was obvious was how friendly the Americans were, and even more so when they found out we were from a different country. So many people really made an effort to engage us in conversation, whether it was on the street, on trains, in restaurants or in shops. At first I found it really strange because I am undeniably British and us Brits can be rather reserved, but after ten days in New York I grew to love their approach. So much so, I resolved that when I got back to London, I was going to make a point of being as friendly as possible when given the opportunity.

A few weeks after my return, I was on a fairly busy train and there were a couple of seats either side of a middle-aged woman. I thought to myself, 'Right, here's the chance I've been waiting for.' Normally I'd just go ahead and sit in the seat without speaking, but today I decided to make a real effort to be friendly. I strolled over, sat down and said, 'Hey, how's it going?' She looked at me with a slightly confused expression, and smiled politely. That was the end of that conversation. She got off at the next stop. About 20 minutes later, at my stop, I got off the train and walked towards the exit. As I glanced through the window of the next carriage down I saw the woman sitting reading a paper! It's a sad day when you're friendly with someone and they respond by moving carriages.

I guess that's the world we live in. Women tend to think that if a guy is being friendly then they must want either their number or their handbag. I can relate to this, as when I was younger, if a guy approached me it was often because he was trying to steal my phone. Past experiences teach us to unfairly stereotype people, but one of the ways we can change that is by going out of our way to talk to people. We should equally be receptive to people who want to speak to us. Malcolm S. Forbes said that you can easily judge the true character of a man by how he treats those who can do nothing for him. Jesus didn't speak to people because he wanted something in return; he spoke to people because he cared deeply for us and wanted to help as many people as possible. He stood up for those who couldn't stand up for themselves. Taking on that characteristic will really help us make an impact on our culture. I love Lawrence G. Lovasik's words: 'Try to make at least one person happy every day. If you cannot do a kind deed, speak a kind word. If you cannot speak a kind word, think a kind thought.'

Jesus Didn't Have a Comfort Zone

I must admit, being Jesus must be pretty cool. During the summer, my friends and I are normally quite busy so we don't get many opportunities to hang out. But after this busy period, we normally make a point of getting together and catching up. We always have some pretty exciting stories to regale each other with: the places we've been to, the latest trainers in our shoe racks, seeing our favourite artists perform live, updates in our relationship statuses. I reckon if we were 2,000 years older and Jesus was in our crew, he would hands down win the prize for best story every time. 'So Jesus, how you been man? What did you get up to over the last few months?'

'Not much, boys. Did a few miracles and preached a bit. Loads of people turned up to see me do my thing. Imagine Drake at the O2 Arena . . . yeah, bigger crowds than that. So it got quite late and I didn't want to miss *Match of the Day* so I hopped into the boat. Took off my trainers first, though. Didn't want to risk getting water on my Bethlehem Air Maxes.

The disciples followed me into the boat. Judas was blanking me all night; I think he's still upset about the time I beat him on FIFA BC. Anyway, we'd been sailing for a bit and there was no Wi-Fi on the boat so I went for a little nap. Out of nowhere the disciples came in shouting and they woke me up to tell me there's a massive storm and the waves are coming into the boat. Peter was as scared as a mouse; you know what he's like! So I got up and said to the disciples, "Chill, fellas, I got this." Then I turned around, looked at the waves and said, "Relax, I'm trying to sleep," and they stopped there and then. Ha-ha, it was sick. You should have seen the disciples' faces, they were looking at me as if they'd just seen Michael Jackson riding a Segway.'

OK, I'm aware it didn't happen *exactly* like that. Jesus did do some incredibly cool things and, though they would look good on a CV, achieving what he did wouldn't have been a comfortable process. He became the saviour of the world. That journey would have been full of hard work, determination, pain and sometimes loneliness – but that didn't stop him. He stayed faithful through it all and became comfortable with being uncomfortable. He didn't mind being inconvenienced because in everything he did he always saw the bigger picture: God's glorious picture.

I have no doubt in my mind that most of us want the world to be a better place, but bringing about change means being uncomfortable. It means putting others first, it means doing the right thing even when you don't feel like it, it means stepping out in faith and trusting God so you can do whatever is needed to see the love of God take its place within our society. Legendary boxer Muhammad Ali once said that he hated every minute of training but he'd rather suffer now and live the rest of his life as a champion. He made himself uncomfortable so that his future could be comfortable. God has placed something so special and unique inside every single one of us, but sadly a lot of us give up when we come up against unexpected and challenging times.

Romans 5.3–4 says this:

We can rejoice, too, when we run into problems and trials, for we know that they help us develop endurance. And endurance develops strength of character, and character strengthens our confident hope of salvation. And this hope will not lead to disappointment. (NLT)

These verses have pretty much got me through my career as a rapper. Whether it was the time when I couldn't afford to go to the studio, or when not as many people bought my album as I had anticipated, I am often reminded that things don't always go according to plan. This verse reminds me that, ultimately, I will not meet disappointment at the end of this journey. Instead I will develop strength, confidence and hope, which perhaps will inspire others. The sooner we get used to being outside of our comfort zones, the sooner we can have an impact on lives other than our own.

CHAPTER 11

FIGHTING EVIL AND INJUSTICE

Before our wedding, Emma and I decided to go on a pre-marital counselling course with one of the leaders from our church and his wife. The aim of the course was to prepare couples for the challenges and pitfalls that may occur during marriage. We found it incredibly helpful because it not only made us think about how we could care for each other in the best way possible, it also encouraged us to talk about all aspects of marriage in depth so that we were prepared for life after we tied the knot. One observation that came out of those sessions was that I struggled to communicate my true feelings and, as a result, I had the tendency to be quite passive. There are a few unappealing words that could be used to describe being passive, including lifeless, insensitive, cold, inactive and unresponsive.

Growing up I struggled to express my feelings externally, so it became a habit for me to do so internally. I told myself that every situation wasn't a big deal and I just needed to get over it, so I would end up never dealing with anything properly. I developed an apathetic attitude and I shied away from difficult conversations. Whenever I had a disagreement or conflict with someone I'd always be the first to back down, but it wasn't because I was trying to do the right thing. It was because I couldn't be bothered to have a mature discussion. I used to feel as though it wasn't worth the hassle; I'd often say sorry without meaning it so I could get out of the conversation.

I've come to realise that this isn't the best way to go about things. I kept sweeping stuff under the carpet – and all that happened was I got a bumpy carpet. I thought I was dealing with my issues quickly but all I was doing by holding back was storing them at the back of my mind. I began to grow bitter about all the unresolved problems I had never spoken up about. I couldn't stand being around certain people, for example, and I began to subconsciously hold grudges. That wasn't going to be healthy for my marriage or my life in general.

Emma encouraged me to open up and gradually I began to talk more. I learned that speaking to someone when I felt down made me feel better. I discovered that saying sorry without meaning it, just to end a disagreement, did more harm than good, and having a conversation with the aim of understanding someone was a much more fulfilling option and made room for sincere apologies. I realised that it's OK to not be OK with something, and speaking about it helps. Having someone who listens, supports me, and wants to help me where possible has opened my eyes and relieved a whole lot of pressure that was building up in my brain. I'm not saying that I'm the perfect communicator now, but I'm not where I used to be. It's important to find someone in your life that you trust so that you can open up. This might be a friend, brother or sister, girlfriend or boyfriend – it doesn't matter who. What's important is that you have someone you can be really honest with.

This increased openness in my relationship with Emma also gave me an outlet to process my reactions to certain painful news stories on TV and in the newspapers. Below are some recent events that really shook me. Not all were well documented in the media, but what they have in common is that none of these atrocities should have happened.

Eric Garner

On 17 July 2014 in New York, Eric Garner was approached by several police officers in front of a beauty supply shop. Police had suspected Garner of selling illegal cigarettes. The whole conversation was filmed on video and Garner can be heard saying: 'Get away. Every time you see me, you want to mess with me. I'm tired of it. It stops today. Why would you . . . ? Everyone standing here will tell you I didn't do nothing. Please just leave me alone.'

Police officer Pantaleo approached Garner from behind and attempted to handcuff him, but Garner flung his arms away, saying, 'Don't touch me, please.' The officer then put Garner in a chokehold behind, something that is not permitted by New York Police Department regulations. He then pulled Garner backwards in an attempt to bring him to the ground, and in the process Eric Garner's head smashed against a glass window. As Garner lay on the ground, five police officers surrounded him and Pantaleo used his hands to push Garner's face into the concrete. Garner can be heard saying, 'I can't breathe,' eleven times while lying face down.

He stopped breathing and an ambulance was called. During the seven minutes it took for the ambulance to arrive, none of the police officers attempted CPR. Garner died an hour later.

Bataclan Attack

On Friday 13 November 2015, three gunmen entered the Bataclan music venue in Paris while a concert was in full swing, and started shooting people at random. Some of the concert-goers managed to escape through the emergency exit door by the stage, but others were trapped. The gunmen started to shoot dead everybody in the bar area. Many people dropped to the floor in panic but that didn't stop the terrorists. They shot at those on the floor and went up to the balcony to shoot more people there. While the gunmen stopped to reload their weapons, people tried to escape through windows and emergency exits. Others found themselves locked in toilets, offices or on rooftops, waiting there for hours until it was all over.

Officers rushed into the building with weapons and bulletproof shields. They shot two of the terrorists and the other one blew himself up. The attack was over but the pain wasn't. Ninety people were killed.

Chibok Kidnapping

On the night of 15 April 2014, 276 girls were kidnapped from their school in Chibok, Nigeria. Islamist militant group Boko Haram walked into the school claiming to be armed guards, and they told the girls to get out of the school immediately and follow them. Many students were taken away in trucks and Boko Haram burned houses in the surrounding area too.

More than 50 schoolgirls managed to escape, and a further 21 Chibok girls were freed after negotiations with Boko Haram in 2016, but the rest remain captured. The Islamist militants have been terrorising north-east Nigeria for almost five years. They do not believe girls should be educated, and because of this have killed, kidnapped and tortured hundreds of girls and women.

Myron Yarde

On 3 April 2016 there was an altercation between a group of young people in New Cross, London. What started out as a fight between a few teenagers ended in 17-year-old Myron

Yarde receiving multiple stab wounds and collapsing in a pool of blood. Paramedics tried to save him at the scene but he died later that evening in hospital.

Myron was an aspiring rapper and well known in the borough of Lewisham. He wasn't a gang member or a known troublemaker, and many described him as a lovely and respectable boy. In the previous year, 19 teenagers were murdered in London; 15 of the deaths were stabbings.

Finding God in the Chaos

As I got more in touch with my emotions, I started to become deeply affected by the examples of evil and injustice that surrounded me. Tragic events would play on my mind for hours – and days – on end and the pain of others became my pain. I began to ask questions. Why is this happening? How can it stop? What can I do to help? God, where are you in this?

I also felt a bit ashamed. Evil and injustice have always plagued our world, so why was it only now that I wanted to get up and do something about it? Well, the honest truth is that I just didn't care enough. I did the easy thing, which was to blame God. I couldn't fathom why bad things happened to good people. However, digging deeper gave me the answers that I needed.

God is first and foremost our loving Father, not our slave master. He gives us free will to make our own decisions and, along with that, he gave us Jesus as the perfect example to follow. However, because we as humans are *imperfect*, we tend to go our own way and have a negative impact on the world. A lot of people are angry at God for things he has never done. God doesn't kill, steal, burgle or sell illegal drugs. People do that. We must make moral choices, and this world can be an overwhelmingly scary place because many of us make the wrong ones.

Seeing the One

Growing up, I saw and read about so much bad news that I became desensitised to it. Racism, sexism, terrorism and every other ism and schism – it was all chucked in my face so often that I stopped *seeing the one*. What I mean by this is that each news story had lost its individual impact and I couldn't comprehend every headline as a real event that happened in a real place, to real people, with real lives. But when I started to picture my loved ones and family members in the horrible situations I read about, my thought pattern changed dramatically. Hearing about a war in Syria on the news makes you think, 'That's really bad'. Hearing about a war in Syria that your mother, father, brother, sister or friend is caught up in makes you think, 'That's *really* bad . . . and how do we make it stop now?' Seeing the one means always to put yourself in the shoes of the individual. For example, racism is bad, but when you put yourself in the shoes of an individual who has received racist abuse, you tend to be more understanding and compassionate.

God wants us to have the 'how do we make it stop now?' view on a regular basis, and not just if it's directly affecting *our* lives. We need to stand with the lonely, the oppressed, the homeless, the war-torn, the orphans, the refugees, the hungry, the afraid, the anxious; the list goes on. Micah 6 contains one of my favourite Bible verses. God has asked Micah, one of God's prophets, to speak to the people on his behalf: 'He's already made it clear how to live and what to do. What God is looking for in men and women is quite simple. Do what is right, love mercy, and walk humbly with God' (Micah 6.8).

I'm fully aware that we are none of us superhuman. Masses of issues plague this world and it's impossible for one person to be contagiously passionate about *all* of them. We don't have the capacity or the resources to do so, but it's important to know that even though we can't do everything, we can do something.

What am I doing? That's the question I had to ask myself and the answer was fairly simple. I had to care. When you care about something enough, you're not only sympathetic, you're empathetic. Sympathy is feeling sorry for someone but empathy is understanding what someone is going through and sharing a person's feelings. The result of caring is action, and there are three things I believe people can do if they want to battle the wickedness of this world.

Speak Out

One thing that bothers me is the way that young black men are often perceived in society. I remember in year seven being in an English lesson and my friends and I were messing about and not concentrating. The teacher got frustrated and said that the next person to do anything silly would have to step outside. As she turned round to write on the board, someone in the class fake coughed and everyone started. The teacher couldn't work out who the culprit was, so she sent five of the liveliest kids outside, including me. My friend, a white person, said, 'Miss, it wasn't me!' She replied, 'I don't care, step outside, please.'

I said, 'Miss, it wasn't me!' in the exact tone, volume and manner as my friend, but her response to me was, 'Stop being so aggressive.' While I am not perfect, and at times I have lost my temper, I have rarely become aggressive and I certainly wasn't aggressive in this scenario.

I strongly believe that young black men are sometimes feared because of the way the media has portrayed them. Since the days of slavery, the narrative of the predatory black man has been used to instil fear. Media images and headlines paint pictures of angry criminals, drug dealers, unemployable and hypersexual members of society. It would be understandable if statistics showed young black men to be more dangerous than other races, but they don't. Am I overreacting, or is there any truth in these prejudices? It's up for debate, but all I know is that all this negative information used to stay in my head. Over time I've realised the importance of sharing my thoughts and feelings. Even though I don't have the answers, it frees me to know that I'm not brushing my issues or perceived social injustices under the carpet. Doing that definitely won't help any situation improve.

You might feel strongly about poverty, human trafficking, climate change or any other worthy cause. Whatever it is, having open, honest discussions around these topics increases knowledge for everyone involved and may lead to strategies that will help solve the problem. Talking through your thoughts and sharing them with another person is like releasing a pressure valve in your head. Switch it on once in a while.

Act

A few years ago, a charity called Compassion came to my church to give a presentation about their work. Compassion work in Africa, Asia, Central America and South America with the aim of bringing children out of poverty. They work with local churches to match the most at-risk children with loving sponsors. The sponsor pays a set amount per month to supply their sponsored child with access to education, health checks and the care of a local Compassion project. They're passionate about giving children the opportunity to escape a life of poverty and live life to the full.

When I heard their presentation, I remember thinking, 'That's really cool'. The truth is that many people would think the same, but how many would *act*? At the time, I was doing a lot of work in the community with young people and was heavily involved with the youth group at my church; I felt I was already doing 'my bit' for society. Although I was passionate about young people, and of course poverty was awful, I believed that someone else would care more about it than I did, and they would sponsor a child and everything would be OK.

However, I then had a bit of an epiphany and thought to myself, 'Imagine if everyone thought like that? Oh, someone else will do it, so I don't need to.' No one would do anything! Poverty seems like such a huge problem, and often when we face huge problems we can think that our little bit would be so insignificant. I felt that sponsoring one child wasn't going to make a difference because there would still be thousands in poverty. Well, to me it may have felt like nothing, but to the child I eventually sponsored it was everything. To me it meant having one less Nando's meal a month; for the child I sponsored it meant breaking the cycle of poverty for life.

I was booked to perform at a show in India, which is where my sponsored child lives. The day after the show I had some spare time so I went along to the shelter to visit her. Having the privilege to eat with her and play with her was quite an emotional experience and one I will cherish for a long time. It made me realise that my contribution to her isn't just a direct debit; it's actually making a real difference in her life. We must not be blind to the trouble that exists in this world. It is a privilege to support justice.

Pray

On 22 December 2012 I received a text with news that knocked me for six and completely broke my heart. A friend of mine had been found at the bottom of a block of flats in east London. He had taken his own life. I was shell-shocked because he seemed like such a happy person, and had such a great future ahead of him. I wish he'd known his value and I wish he'd known that no matter what trials we go through, there is always a light at the end of the tunnel.

At that point I couldn't talk to anyone, and I couldn't act because the devastating damage had already been done. The only thing I felt comfortable doing was praying. It wasn't a long prayer. I said something like, 'God, comfort his family, and give peace to everyone hurting right now.'

For me personally, prayer has often been my only option. Feeling completely helpless leaves me in a miserable state and it has comforted me to know during troubled times that I have someone bigger than it all. Talking about pain, sorrow, injustice and evil is important, and acting on those issues to make a fairer world is even better, but in certain situations we don't have the power to do anything. For me, that's when prayer comes in.

When I was younger, I learned about a few heroes: Father Christmas, the Tooth Fairy, the Easter Bunny and Jesus. As I've got older I've succumbed to the fact that Father Christmas, the Tooth Fairy and the Easter Bunny probably aren't real (sorry for the spoiler). There have also been times when people have tried to tell me that Jesus isn't real, or isn't who he says he is, but I've never bought it. I've always felt the sense that he's a genuine Saviour who cares about me and hears my prayers.

This influences a lot of my music. One of my most popular songs is an urban take on the classic hymn 'Nothing but the blood'. The third verse is probably the favourite piece I've written throughout my whole career. It explains just how much of a Saviour God has been for me and how having him in my corner has given me unmatchable hope. Here it is.

And so I'm here
And I'm still standing by His grace, it disappeared
All of my failures, all my shame, now I see clear
And that's because no other name has brought me near
And I can't wait to see His face I'm pressing on
All my mistakes they are erased and now I'm strong
It's like the judge has closed the case I can move on
And yeah I've moved from place to place,
But now I found where I belong.

CONCLUSION
BE THE SURPRISE

A while ago I was in Los Angeles performing. I had a day off so decided to visit a local church. I heard a guy called Erwin McManus speak and he said something that inspired me greatly.

> Be the human surprise. People expect you to be judgemental, selfish and condemning. What they don't expect is for you to be joyful, caring, gracious, selfless, and to give to those in need. When you wake up in the morning, choose to see beauty and walk in God's purpose for your life. If you do, you'll surprise the world.

It's time for *us* to surprise the world. God wants to use *you* and he has a purpose for you to influence culture. Don't settle for how things currently are, and don't let others dictate how and what you should be. We can be part of God's plan to bring hope to a hopeless generation.

Spend time with people who aren't like you – who don't think like you, act like you, speak like you or eat like you; who don't want the same things as you or have the same needs as you. It will open up your mind.

Let's flip the script, demonstrate another way to live and find freedom in going against the grain.

The Gospel of John serves as great inspiration for us. Jesus' work on earth is done and he's about to go to the cross. He knows what's going to happen so he gathers the disciples together for one last time to pray with them. Just before Jesus is arrested, he leaves his friends with undeniable hope. 'I have told you these things, so that in me you may have peace. In this world you will have trouble. But take heart! I have overcome the world' (John 16.33, NIV).

I love it that the words 'take heart' are followed by an exclamation mark. It isn't just a throwaway comment; it's a call to action! What kind of world would we live in if Martin Luther King didn't take heart? How many people would be unfairly locked up in prison if Nelson Mandela didn't take heart? How many more people would be living in poverty today if Mother Teresa didn't take heart? All these cultural heroes are with us no more, so who's going to carry the baton now? I believe we can. Yes, we will face very real challenges, but take heart! Jesus has overcome them all.

This verse fills me with such peace and hope. I can't let fear get the upper hand. Regardless of what the evil in this world throws at us, God can and will protect us. I am determined to stand up for what is right and not succumb to the status quo of culture today. Join me. Let's dare to be unpopular.

ALLO, MATE . . .

Writing a book is definitely one of the hardest things I've done. It took me a year to finish it and I'd be lying if I said there weren't times I felt like giving up. (I couldn't, though, because my publishers might have sued me.)

I have to thank my head teacher at primary school, Mrs Aanonson. I was pretty naughty at school but when you weren't telling me off in your office you were telling me how good my writing was. I loved writing essays in English class because you made me believe I was good at it. Your encouraging words helped lead me into a career of writing lyrics and now, a book. Thanks, Miss.

My wifey, Emma. I love you, babes. Thanks for being patient while I was writing this and spurring me on. Also thanks for telling me what I wasn't allowed to say in this book ☺.

Mum and Dad. We're quite a small family but you taught us to dream big. I'm grateful for all the sacrifices you made and I hope you're proud.

Joel, I thought of you a lot while writing this book, lil bro. I'm happy that you've learnt from most of the mistakes I made and you're always striving to do better and be better. Michaela, thanks for encouraging me to be myself and to feel comfortable in my own skin. Sophia, cheers for always being there when I need you.

Sarah (the OG), thanks for reading over my chapters, correcting my grammatical mistakes, and being real and honest with what didn't make sense.

Joe Widdowson, Daisy Morgan, Nick Brewer, Jordan Spence, Naomi Scott, Ben Lindsay, Jake Isaac, Barney Isukali, Jake Toppin, Sone Aluko, Chisom Chigbo, Phil Kyei, Glen Templeman, Chloe Templeman, Ben Hale, William Adoasi, Matty Smith, Jay Richards and Carlene Noel. You lot keep me grounded. Thanks for the advice, the support, and for telling me what I need to hear, not what I want to hear.

Thanks to my team for supporting another project. Wayne Hermz, Doug Ross, Chris Panayi, Luke Williams, Tom Ruddock, James McGuiness, Robbie Semmence, Luke English, JimmyJames, Kevin Hudson and Christophe Pierre. You've all been consistently great for years now.

Thanks to the new members of the squad also. Juliet Trickey, Olivia Carson, Mark Read and everyone at SPCK. It's been super fun working on this with you.

To everyone who listens to my music or follows me on Facebook, Instagram, Snapchat, Twitter or whatever else. I'm living a life I never would have dreamed of so thanks for helping to make it possible. My prayer is to see each and every one of you become the best possible versions of yourselves.

Carnell King, Noah Redman and Harrison Cosstick. You are just three examples of the kind of multi-talented and determined young people I'm blessed to know. I think you'll go on to make the world a better place. I wrote this book for people like you. Always strive for better and believe God for bigger.

Last but not least, thank you, Jesus. If you never do another thing for me ever again, you've already done more than enough.

ABOUT THE AUTHOR

Guvna B is a double MOBO award-winning grime/rap artist from London. He became the first rapper in UK history to top the Official Christian & Gospel Albums Chart. He holds a record for mainstream success too: his album *Secret World* was the highest-selling 'clean' rap album of 2015.

As well as sharing stages with the likes of Tinie Tempah, Wretch 32, Kirk Franklin and Lecrae, his story has been covered by the BBC, Sky News and Channel 4. He has worked with artists such as Matt Redman, Hillsong Music, Nick Brewer, Michelle Williams of Destiny's Child and Keisha Buchanan.

In creating output, the business and journalism graduate draws from his faith, personal experiences and observations made while living in and around the fast-paced, gritty environment of London's streets. Guvna B, an avid West Ham fan, hopes to inspire young people to reach their full God-given potential.